the documents of modern art

wittenborn, schultz, inc., new york

beyond painting

max **ernst**

The

Documents

of

Modern

Art   *director*, Robert Motherwell

Max Ernst : Beyond Painting

And other Writings by the Artist and his Friends

Wittenborn, Schultz, Inc.   1948

New York

Acknowledgements:

The publishers and the director acknowledge their indebtedness to the artist
for aid and advice in preparing the text and illustrations, to Dorothea Tanning
and Ralph Manheim for their translations, to Arp, André Breton,
Nicolas Calas, Paul Éluard, Julien Levy, Matta, Georges Ribemont-Dessaignes,
Tristan Tzara and their publishers for permission to include their
contributions, to private and public collections for their
collaboration, to the photographers, and to Bernard Karpel for his bibliography.

Prefatory Note:

The struggle of most modern painters takes place in their studios, their structural devices are plastic means for reproducing dramas that happen within the self. Their assault upon society is by indirection, through contrasting the subjectively real with the conventional. In contrast, Max Ernst is among the few consequential modern painters whose concern is directly with the external world, with the world of social events and institutions — the Church, political repression, erotic enslavement. His work is filled with ironies and cruelties, sarcasms and satires. For example, his Natural History *is an act of revolt projected from the level of poetry against the rational approach to nature as we find it in science books. It is a poetic act. And one specifically surrealist.*

I for one am not in the least disturbed by the fact that modes of expression that mean much to me . . . minimization of the role of objects, tactility, flatness, abstract plasticity . . . are ignored or even undermined by Ernst's painting. His subject matter is contemporary history, for him man is essentially a historical creature; Ernst has to employ images, objects, all the paraphernalia of the external world; he warns, criticizes, jeers, prophesies, lays bare suppressed phantasies. His vision is that "nothing is in order," that the order out there has nothing to do with a truly human order, that we are victims of history. His art depends on the sense of a vicious past.

To the American mind nothing could be more alien than such a contest with the past. Such images as a black mass, a bloody nun, an invader from the east cannot arouse deep feelings in most of us. Time gives objects and images their qualities of love and hate; generations of connotations, associations, sense experiences are what make the past. But for better or worse, most Americans have no sensation of being either elevated or smothered by the past; most of us (or our ancestors) came here in order to cease to deal with the past. Con-

v

sciously abandoning the past is the essentially American creative act; we painters here remain indifferent to the objects surrounding us. Our emotional interest is not in the external world, but in creating a world of our own, and it is precisely those artists here who are not "conscious" who behave as if America had a useable past.

It is from this reasoning that we can account for the fact that objectless painting, that is, various modes of abstraction, appeals more to most modern American painters than surrealism. But the American experience is a small part of the story of modern art which, with its variety, its contradictions and dilemmas, its heroic monsters and monstrous victims, is a reflection of the general human situation in our time. Human reality appears in it as constituted of bitter and relentless struggles over each person's image of the world . . . struggles located largely on unconscious and symbolic planes of action. What absorbs me in the history of modern art is the ingenuity and inventiveness, the wit and subtlety, the implacability and force with which each modern painter has carried out his assaults upon the conventional world.

Like every consequential modern painter, Max Ernst has enforced his own madness on the world, which has to submit, since madness that moves and creates is a liberation, in contrast to the sterile madness of people tied to conventions . . .

These reflections support my spontaneous interest in the universe of Max Ernst. They do not account for my personal affection for him during the five or six years I have known him, the natural affection of a younger painter who has been treated in a friendly, generous, fraternal way by a mature painter and personality whose freedom in action, gesture, and speech makes his company always lively and liberating. But even one not acquainted with him, and committed, as I am, to quite another vision in painting, would inevitably be brought, some time or other, to contemplate his message. His work represents the assault of his poetics on the conventional, including many of the conventions of modern plasticity.   Robert Motherwell   June, 1948

Biographical Note:

1891	Born at Brühl, near Cologne (Rhineland), of a strict Catholic bourgeois family. Paintings in oil on diapers.
1893	Changes to pencil on paper.
1900	Oil on canvas and other materials.
1898–1914	Grade school and high school in Brühl; then at Bonn University. (Never attended an art school.)
1913	Exhibited at the "Erster Deutscher Herbstsalon," Berlin. First sojourn in Paris.
1914–1918	Boredom of military life and warfare. Very little work.
1919	Cologne. Co-founder with Baargeld and Arp of "Dada W/3" (i.e., "Weststupidia" divided by three). Co-editor of the review, *Die Schammade*.
1919–1921	Dada exhibitions in Cologne: at the "Kölnischer Kunstverein" and at the "Brauhaus Winter" and "Das Junge Rheinland" (Düsseldorf).
1920	First one-man collage show in Paris. Preface by André Breton.
1921	Historic meeting in the Tyrol with Arp, Tzara and Breton. Contributed to the magazine, *Dada au grand Air* ("Dada in the great out-of-doors") or *Der Sängerkrieg in Tirol* ("The singing contest in the Tyrol"). Friendship with Paul Eluard; illustrations for his book, *Répétitions*.
1922	Second meeting in the Tyrol with Arp, Eluard, Tzara, Josephson and others. *Les Malheurs des Immortels*, in collaboration with Eluard.
	Paris. Contributed to *Littérature* (the magazine edited by André Breton and Philippe Soupault). Experiments with automatism, with Breton, Crevel, Desnos, Eluard, Picabia, Péret, Ribemont-Dessaignes, Man Ray, Vitrac, and others.
1922–1924	"Woman, Old Man and Flower," "Revolution by Night," "Au Rendez-vous des Amis," "La Belle Jardinière," and other works.
1924	Co-founder of the surrealist movement. Contributed to *La Révolution Surréaliste*, and other publications.
1926–1939	One-man exhibitions in Paris, Brussels, London, Zurich, Madrid, Berlin, New York, Los Angeles, etc.
1926	*Histoire Naturelle*, published by Jeanne Bucher, Paris (first results of "frottage").
1927	Monte Carlo. Stage sets, in collaboration with Miró, for "Romeo and Juliet," produced by Diaghileff.

1929	*La Femme 100 Têtes*, published by Carrefour, Paris.
1930	*Rêve d'une Petite Fille qui Voulut Entrer au Carmel*, published by Carrefour.
1933	Placed on Nazi black-list.
1934	*Une Semaine de Bonté*, published by Jeanne Bucher. Sculptures in the garden of Giacometti, Maloja, Switzerland.
1936	*Au delà de la Peinture*, published by Cahiers d'Art, Paris.
1937	Stage sets for Alfred Jarry's *Ubu Enchaîné*, Comédie des Champs Elysées, Paris.
1938–1939	Sculptures and murals for the artist's house at St. Martin d'Ardèche, in the south of France.
1939–1940	Decalcomanic discoveries made between internments in concentration camps (French).
1941–1945	New York. One-man exhibitions in New York, Chicago, New Orleans, Washington, D.C. Special number of *View Magazine* (1942) devoted to Max Ernst. Co-editor of VVV (with David Hare, André Breton and Marcel Duchamp).
1945	Retrospective exhibition at Galerie Denise René, Paris.
	Contributions to Hans Richters' film, *Dreams That Money Can Buy*.
1946	Sedona, Arizona. Building, sculpturing, painting, writing, and . . . last but not least . . . loving (Dorothea).

Contents:

List of illustrations of Max Ernst's work:

(The medium oil refers to oil paintings on canvas unless otherwise stated. When two dates are given, the first one is that preferred by the artist.)

xi

Max Ernst: *Beyond Painting and other Writings*

Beyond Painting 1. *History of a Natural History*

". . . it is like the tinkling of the bell, which makes one hear that which one imagines."
Leonardo da Vinci. (*Treatise on Painting*)

From 5 to 7 years

I see before me a panel, very rudely painted with wide black lines on a red ground, representing false mahogany and calling forth associations of organic forms (menacing eye, long nose, great head of a bird with thick black hair, etc.).

In front of the panel, a glossy black man is making gestures, slow, comical and, according to my memories of a very obscure epoch, joyously obscene. This rogue of a fellow wears the turned-up moustaches of my father.

After having executed some leaps in slow motion, legs spread, knees drawn up, torso bent forward, he smiles and draws from the pocket of his trousers a fat crayon in a soft material which I find I cannot describe more precisely. He sets to work: panting violently he hurriedly traces the black lines on the panel of false mahogany. He quickly imparts to it new forms, forms which are at once surprising and abject. He accentuates the resemblance to ferocious or viscous animals to such a point that he extracts from it living creatures that fill me with horror and anguish. Content with his art, the fellow tosses his creations in the air, then gathers them in a kind of vase which he paints, intentionally, on the inside. He whirls the contents of the vase by stirring it, faster and faster, with his fat crayon. The vase itself, in whirling, becomes a top. The crayon becomes a whip. Now I realize that this strange painter is my father. He wields the whip with all his force and accompanies his movements with terrible gasps of breath, comparable to the snorts of an enormous and enraged steam-engine. With fiendish passion he causes the top to whirl and leap around my bed, that abominable top which contains all the horrors that my

3

father is capable of evoking in an amiable panel of false mahogany by means of his frightful soft crayon.

One day, at the age of puberty, in examining the question of how my father had conducted himself in the night of my conception, there rose in me, as if in response to this question of filial respect, precise and irrefutable, the memory of that vision of half sleep that I had forgotten. For a long time afterward I was unable to disengage myself from a quite unfavorable impression of my father's conduct on the occasion of my conception, an impression perhaps unreasonable and unjust, but carefully thought over. . . .

At the age of puberty

The well-known game of purely optical representations which obsesses us in half-sleep quickly becomes a procession of normally clad men and women which departs from a distant horizon toward my bed. Before arriving, the participants separate: the women pass to the right, the men to the left. Curious, I lean toward the right so that not one face shall escape me. Moreover, I am struck by the extreme youth of all these women; and later by the fact that the persons in question are always the same, only the head changing a little, the identity never. In scrutinizing them carefully, face by face, I realize my error: among these women many are of a "certain age," some really old and only two or three very young, perhaps 18 years of age, the age expedient to my puberty.

I am too occupied by the women to give any attention to those passing on the men's side. But *I know without seeing* that I shall now commit the contrary error: All these gentlemen begin by frightening me with their precocious senility and their remarkable ugliness, but upon close examination only my father, among all these, bears the traits of an old man.

January 1925

I see myself lying in my bed and, standing at my feet a tall slender woman dressed in a very red gown. The gown is transparent, the woman also. I am ravished by the surprising elegance of her bone structure. I am tempted to pay her a compliment.

The 10th of August, 1925

Botticelli did not like landscape painting. He felt that it was "a kind of short and mediocre investigation." He says with contempt that "by throwing a sponge soaked with different colors against a wall one makes a spot in which may be seen a beautiful landscape." That statement brought him a severe admonition from his colleague, Leonardo da Vinci:

"He (Botticelli) is right; in such a daub one may certainly find bizarre inventions. I mean to say that he who is disposed to gaze attentively at this spot

4

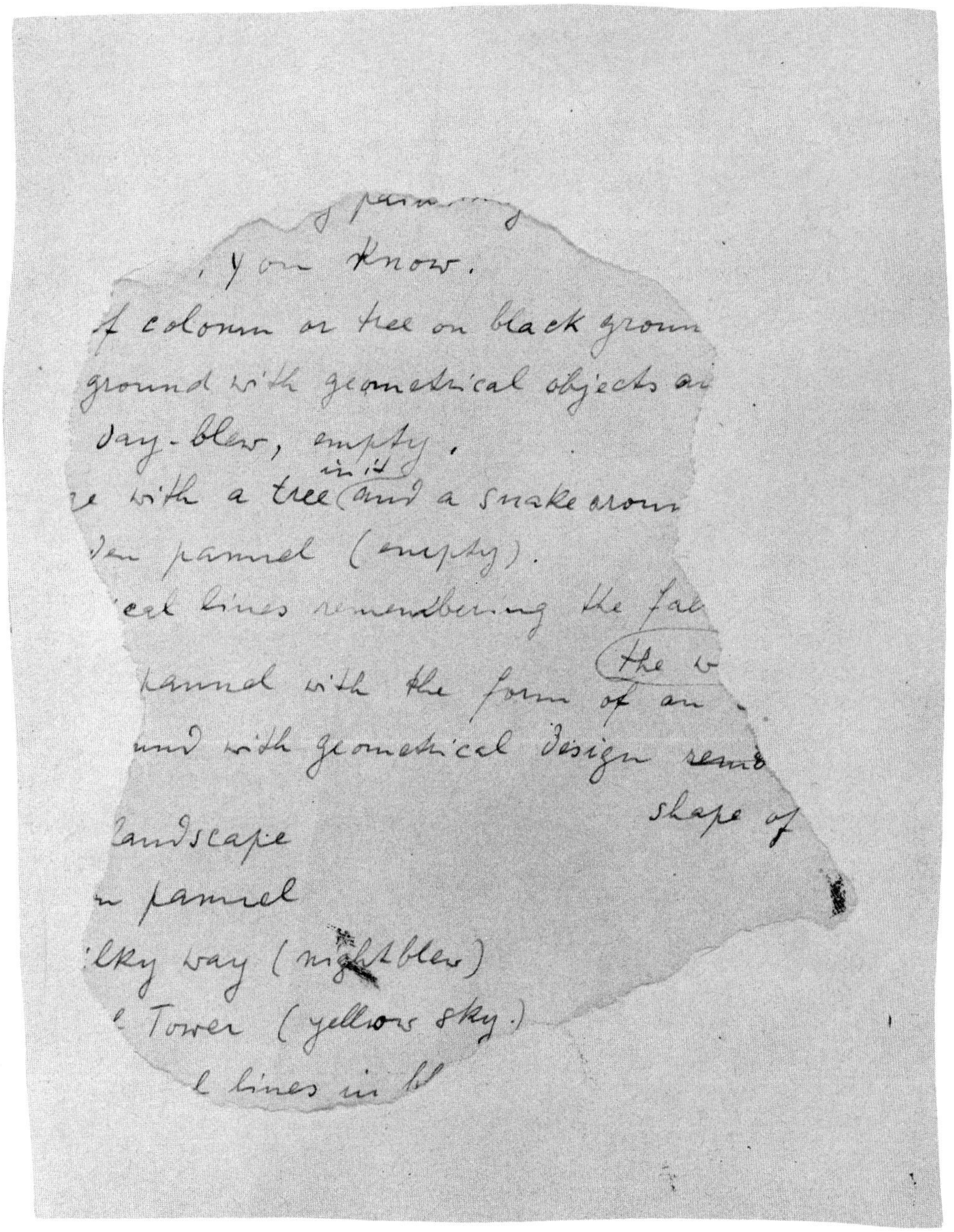
f painting
, you know.
f colomn or tree on black groun
ground with geometrical objects a
day-blew, empty.
e with a tree in it and a snake aroun
den pannel (empty).
ical lines remembering the fa
the w
pannel with the form of an
und with geometrical design remi
shape of
landscape
n pannel
lky way (night blew)
e Tower (yellow sky.)
l lines in bl

Manuscript Page

Max Ernst's Favorite

Poets *Of The* Past Painters

NOVALIS

Coleridge

CRABBE

Browning
BLAKE

LAUTREAMONT

HÖLDERLIN

JARRY

APOLLINAIRE

BAUDELAIRE

RIMBAUD

CARROLL

Heine

HUGO

Solomon

Goethe
ARNIM

Shakespeare

POE

Whitman

SEURAT

GRUENEWALD

BREUGHEL

BOSCH

Perugino

VanGogh

CHIRICO

VINCI

Cranach

Cossa

CRIVELLI

CARPACCIO

UGGELLO

Rousseau

TURA

COSIMO

FRANCESCA

Altdorfer

N. M. DEUTSCH

may discern therein some human heads, various animals, a battle, some rocks, the sea, clouds, groves, and a thousand other things — it is like the tinkling of the bell which makes one hear what one imagines. But though this stain serves to suggest some ideas it does not teach one how to finish any part of the painting. And the above-mentioned painter makes very bad landscapes. To be universal and to please varying tastes it is necessary that in the same composition may be found some very dark passages and others of a gently lighted penumbra. It is not to be despised, in my opinion, if, after gazing fixedly at the spot on the wall, the coals in the grate, the clouds, the flowing stream, if one remembers some of their aspects; and if you look at them carefully you will discover some quite admirable inventions. Of these the genius of the painter may take full advantage, to compose battles of animals and of men, of landscapes or monsters, of devils and other fantastic things which bring you honor. In these confused things genius becomes aware of new inventions, but it is necessary to know well (how to draw) all the parts that one ignores, such as the parts of animals and the aspects of landscape, rocks and vegetation."

(from Treatise on Painting.)

On the tenth of August, 1925, an insupportable visual obsession caused me to discover the technical means which have brought a clear realization of this lesson of Leonardo. Beginning with a memory of childhood (related above) in the course of which a panel of false mahogany, situated in front of my bed, had played the role of optical *provocateur* of a vision of half-sleep, and finding myself one rainy evening in a seaside inn, I was struck by the obsession that showed to my excited gaze the floor-boards upon which a thousand scrubbings had deepened the grooves. I decided then to investigate the symbolism of this obsession and, in order to aid my meditative and hallucinatory faculties, I made from the boards a series of drawings by placing on them, at random, sheets of paper which I undertook to rub with black lead. In gazing attentively at the drawings thus obtained, "the dark passages and those of a gently lighted penumbra," I was surprised by the sudden intensification of my visionary capacities and by the hallucinatory succession of contradictory images superimposed, one upon the other, with the persistence and rapidity characteristic of amorous memories.

My curiosity awakened and astonished, I began to experiment indifferently and to question, utilizing the same means, all sorts of materials to be found in my visual field: leaves and their veins, the ragged edges of a bit of linen, the brushstrokes of a "modern" painting, the unwound thread from a spool, etc. There my eyes discovered human heads, animals, a battle that ended with a kiss (*the bride of the wind*) rocks, *the sea and the rain, earthquakes,* the *sphinx in her stable,* the *little tables around the earth,* the *palette of Caesar, false positions,* a *shawl of frost flowers,* the *pampas.*

7

Blows of whips and threads of lava, fields of honor, inundations and seismic plants, fans, the plunge of the chestnut tree.

The *lightning flashes under fourteen years of age, the vaccinated bread, the conjugal diamonds, the cuckoo, origin of the pendulum, the feast of death, the wheel of light.*

A system of solar money.

The habits of leaves, the fascinating cypress.

Eve, the only one who remains to us.

Under the title *Natural History* I have brought together the first results obtained by the procedure of *frottage* (rubbing), from *The Sea and the Rain* to *Eve, the Only One Who Remains to Us.* (Published in 1926, under the direction of Jeanne Bucher.)

I insist on the fact that the drawings thus obtained lost more and more, through a series of suggestions and transmutations that offered themselves spontaneously — in the manner of that which passes for hypnagogic visions — the character of the material interrogated (the wood, for example) and took on the aspect of images of an unhoped-for precision, probably of a sort which revealed the first cause of the obsession, or produced a simulacrum of that cause.

From 1925 to the present

The procedure of *frottage*, resting thus upon nothing more than the intensification of the irritability of the mind's faculties by appropriate technical means, excluding all conscious mental guidance (of reason, taste, morals), reducing to the extreme the active part of that one whom we have called, up to now, the "author" of the work, this procedure is revealed by the following to be the real equivalent of that which is already known by the term *automatic writing*. It is as a spectator that the author assists, indifferent or passionate, at the birth of his work and watches the phases of its development. Even as the role of the poet, since the celebrated *lettre de voyant* of Rimbaud, consists in writing according to the dictates of that which articulates itself in him, so the role of the painter is to pick out and *project that which sees itself in him.*[1] In finding myself more and more engrossed in this activity (passivity) which later came to be called "critical paranoia,"[2] and in adapting to the technical means of painting (for example: the scraping of pigments upon a ground pre-

---

1. Vasari relates that Piero di Cosimo sometimes sat plunged in contemplation of a wall upon which certain sick persons had formed the habit of spitting. Out of these stains he formed equestrian battles, fantastic towns and the most magnificent landscapes. He did the same with the clouds of the sky.

2. This rather pretty term (and one which will probably have some success because of its paradoxical content) seems to me to be subject to precaution inasmuch as the notion of paranoia is employed there in a sense which doesn't correspond to its medical meaning. I prefer, on the other hand, the proposition of Rimbaud: "The poet becomes a *seer*, by a long, immense and conscious disorder of all the senses."

pared in colors and placed on an uneven surface) the procedure of *frottage* which seemed applicable at first only to drawing, and in striving more and more to restrain my own active participation in the unfolding of the picture and, finally, by widening in this way the active part of the mind's hallucinatory faculties I came to assist *as spectator* at the birth of all my works, from the tenth of August, 1925,[3] memorable day of the discovery of *frottage*. A man of "ordinary constitution" (I employ here the words of Rimbaud), I have done everything to render my soul monstrous.[4] Blind swimmer, I have made myself see. *I have seen*. And I was surprised and enamoured of what I *saw*, wishing to identify myself with it.

In a country the color of a *pigeon's breast* I acclaimed the flight of *1,000,000 doves*. I saw them invade the *forests*, black with desires, and the *walls* and *seas* without end.

I saw an *ivy leaf float upon the ocean* and I felt a *very gentle earthquake*. I saw a *pale, white dove, flower of the desert. She refused to understand. Along the length of a cloud* a superb man and woman *danced the Carmagnole of love*. The Dove *closed herself in her wings* and swallowed the key forever.

A string lying on my table made me see a number of *young men trampling upon their mother*, while several *young girls* amused themselves with *beautiful poses*.

Some exceedingly beautiful women cross a river, crying. A man, walking on the water, takes a young girl by the hand and jostles another. Some persons of a rather reassuring aspect — in fact, *they had lain too long in the forest* — made their *savage gestures* only *to be charming*. Someone said: "*The immobile father*."

It was then that I saw myself, *showing my father's head to a young girl*. The earth quaked but slightly.

I decided to erect a *monument to the birds*.

It was *the beautiful season*. It was the time of *serpents, earth worms, plume-flowers, scale-flowers, tubular flowers*. It was the time when *the forest flew away and the flowers struggled under the water*. The time of the *circumflex Medusa*.

In 1930, after having composed with violence and method my story, *The Hundred-Headed Woman* (Woman Without a Head),[5] I was visited nearly every day by the *Superior of the birds* named *Loplop*, my private phantom,

3. With the exception of *The Virgin Spanking the Infant Jesus* (1926), picture-manifesto, painted after an idea of André Breton.

4. "Monstrous," in this sense, is meant to convey the idea of nobility, greatness, immensity. (Translator's note.)

5. In the French the title is *La Femme 100 Têtes*. It is an excellent example of the "play on words" habit of this period of dada, surrealism and particularly the author. When spelled the title is *The Hundred-Headed Woman*, when pronounced it is *The Woman Without a Head* as well. (Translator's note.)

9

attached to my person. He presented me with a *heart in a cage*, the *sea in a cage, two petals, three leaves, a flower and a young girl*. Also, *the man of the black eggs and the man with the red cape*. On a beautiful autumn afternoon he told me that one day *he had invited a Lacedemonian to come and listen to a man who imitated the nightingale quite perfectly. The Lacedemonian replied: "I have often heard the nightingale herself."* One evening he told me some jokes which didn't make me laugh: "*Joke: it would be better not to reward a beautiful deed at all than to reward it badly*. A soldier had lost both arms in a battle. His colonel offered him a five dollar bill. The soldier responded: "No doubt you think, sir, that I have lost only a pair of gloves."

I had already said "Bonjour" to Satan in 1928. An unavowed old man was burdened at that time with a bundle of clouds on his back while a white lace flower, its neck pierced by a stone, trembled quietly as it sat upon a tambourine. Why am I not this charming flower? Why do I always change myself into an earthquake, the ace of spades, a shadow entering through the doorway?

Somber vision, that of Europe after the rain!

The 24th of December, 1933 I was visited by a young chimera in evening dress.

Eight days later I met a blind swimmer.

A little patience (15 days of waiting) and I should assist in the attirement of the bride. The bride of the wind embraced me in passing by at a swift gallop (simple effect of touch).

I saw the barbarians looking toward the west, barbarians emerging from the forest, barbarians walking toward the west. On my return to the garden of the Hesperides I followed, with a joy that was but poorly concealed, the phases of a battle between two bishops. "It was as beautiful as the chance meeting upon an operating table of a sewing machine and an umbrella." (Lautréamont).

I caressed the lioness of Belfort.
The antipode of the landscape.
A beautiful Rhenish woman.
Whole wheat landscape.
The asparagus of the moon.
The drakes of Mars.
The absolute presence.

Voracious gardens devoured by a vegetation springing from the debris of trapped airplanes.

I saw myself with the head of a kite, a knife in my hand, in the attitude of *The Thinker* of Rodin. But it was actually the liberated attitude of Rimbaud's *Seer*.

I saw with my eyes the nymph Echo.

I saw with my eyes the appearances of things receding, and I felt a calm and ferocious joy. In the measure of my activity (passivity) I contributed to the general overthrow of those values which, in our time, have been considered the most established and secure.

The indicating forest

Enter, enter, have no fear of being blinded. . . .

The field of vision and of action opened up by *frottage* is not limited by the capacity of the mind's faculties of irritability. It far surpasses the limits of artistic and poetic activity. On this subject I could not better explain myself than by quoting the words of André Breton:

"Leonardo's lesson, setting his students to copy in their pictures that which they saw taking shape in the spots on an old wall (each according to his own lights) is far from being understood. The whole passage from subjectivity to objectivity is implicitly resolved there, and the weight of that resolution goes far beyond, in human interest, the weight of inspiration itself. Surrealism has been most particularly concerned with that part of the lesson. Surrealism did not start from there, but rediscovered it on the way and with it, its possibilities of extension to all other domains besides painting. The new associations of images brought forth by the poet, the artist, the scientist, are comparable to it, inasmuch as their creation uses a screen of a particular structure which, concretely, can be either a decrepit wall, a cloud or anything else: a persistent and vague sound carries to the exclusion of all others, the phrase we need to hear. The most striking fact is that an activity of this kind which in order to exist necessitates the unreserved acceptance of a more or less lasting passivity, far from being limited to the sensory world, has been able to penetrate profoundly the moral world. The good luck, the happiness of the scientist or the artist in their *discovery* can only be considered as a particular case, not distinguished in its essence from ordinary human happiness. Some day, man will be able to direct himself if, like the artist, he will consent to reproduce, without changing anything, that which an appropriate screen can offer him in advance of his acts. This screen exists. Every life contains some of these homogeneous entities, of cracked or cloudy appearance, which each of us has only to consider fixedly in order to read his own near future. He should enter the whirlwind, he should retrace the stream of events which, above all others, seemed to him doubtful or obscure and by which he was harassed. There — if his interrogation is worth the effort — all the logical principles will be routed and the powers of the *objective hazard*, making a joke of all probability, will come to his aid. On this screen, everything which man wants to know is written in phosphorescent letters, in letters of *desire*." (from *The Star-Shaped Castle*.)

11. *The Placing Under Whisky-Marine*

> LA MISE SOUS WHISKY MARIN se fait en crême kaki et en 5 anatomies
>
> les dames sont priées d'apporter tous leurs bijoux
>
> VIVE LE SPORT
> AU SANS PAREIL 37 AVENUE KLÉBER PARIS 16e
> du 3 mai au 3 juin 1920
>
> VOUS N'ETES QUE DES ENFANTS
>
> ENTRÉE LIBRE   EXPOSITION DADA   SORTIE FACILE
> mains dans les poches   MAX ERNST   tableau sous le bras
>
> dessins mécanoplastiques plasto-plastiques peintopeintures anaplastiques anatomiques antizymiques aérographiques antiphonaires arrosables et républicains.
>
> comme un seul homme   AU-DELA DE LA PEINTURE   blague dans le coin

Before he became spoiled Aragon wrote:

"When and where did collage first appear? I believe, in spite of the attempts of several dadaists of the first moment, that one must pay homage to Max Ernst for it, at least for that which among the forms of collage, is farthest from the principle of *papier collé:* photographic collage and collage from illustrations. Everything outside of this discovery had the tendency to become generalized, and the German Dada publications, for example, contained collages signed by at least ten authors. However, the success of this procedure depended more upon the astonishment of *knowing the system* than upon the necessity of expressing oneself at any price. Very soon the use of collage was found to be limited to a few men and it is certain that the whole atmosphere of the collages of that time was found to be that of the thought of Max Ernst and Max Ernst only."   (from *A Challenge to Painting*.)

What is collage?

The simple hallucination, after Rimbaud; the placing under whisky-marine,[6] after Max Ernst. It is something like the alchemy of the visual image. THE MIRACLE OF THE TOTAL TRANSFIGURATION OF BEINGS AND OBJECTS WITH OR WITHOUT MODIFICATION OF THEIR PHYSICAL OR ANATOMICAL ASPECT.

"Poetic old-worldliness played a large part in my verbal alchemy.

"I accustomed myself to simple hallucination: I saw quite deliberately a mosque in place of a factory, a drummers' school conducted by angels, carriages on the highways of the sky, a salon at the bottom of a lake; monsters, mysteries, a vaudeville poster raising horrors before my eyes.

"Then I expressed my magic sophisms with the hallucination of words." (Rimbaud: *A Season in Hell.*)

---

6. Whisky-Marine — like aquamarine. A distortion, humorous and very serious at the same time.

12

What is the mechanism of collage?

I am tempted to see in collage the exploitation of the chance meeting of two distant realities on an unfamiliar plane or, to use a shorter term, the culture of systematic displacement and its effects. In the words of André Breton: "Surreality will be the function of our will to recognize completely our own lonely displacement (and it is easily understood that if one were to displace a hand by severing it from an arm, that hand becomes more wonderful as a hand; — and in speaking of the 'lonely displacement' we are not thinking only of the possibility of moving in space)."   (Preface to *The Hundred-Headed Woman.*)

A ready-made reality, whose naive destination has the air of having been fixed, once and for all (a canoe), finding itself in the presence of another and hardly less absurd reality (a vacuum cleaner), in a place where both of them must feel displaced (a forest), will, by this very fact, escape to its naive destination and to its identity; it will pass from its false absolute, through a series of relative values, into a new absolute value, true and poetic: canoe and vacuum cleaner will make love. The mechanism of collage, it seems to me, is revealed by this very simple example. The complete transmutation, followed by a pure act, as that of love, will make itself known naturally *every time the conditions are rendered favorable by the given facts: the coupling of two realities, irreconcilable in appearance, upon a plane which apparently does not suit them.*

Speaking of the procedure of collage in 1920 André Breton tells us: "But the marvelous faculty of reaching two distant realities, without leaving the field of our experience, and, at their coming together, of drawing out a spark; of putting within reach of our senses some abstract figures carrying the same intensity, the same relief as the others; and in depriving ourselves of a system of reference, of displacing ourselves in our own memory — that is what, provisionally, holds us." (Preface to the Max Ernst exhibition, May 1920.) And he adds here these prophetic words: "Who knows if, thus, we are not preparing ourselves to escape some day the principle of identity."

What is the technique of collage?

If it is the plumes that make the plumage it is not the glue that makes the gluing (ce n'est pas la colle qui fait le collage).

One day in the summer of 1929 a painter I knew asked me: "What are you doing these days? Are you working?" I replied: "Yes, I'm making gluings. I'm preparing a book that will be called *La Femme 100 Têtes.*" Then he whispered in my ear: "And what sort of glue do you use?" With that modest air that my contemporaries admire in me I was obliged to confess to him that in most of my collages there wasn't any glue at all. Also that I am not responsible for the term "collage"; that of the fifty-six titles in the catalogue of my exhibition of collages in Paris in 1920, an exhibition which, according to Aragon: ". . . is perhaps the first showing which allows one a glimpse of the resources and the thousand means of an entirely new art — in this city where Picasso has never had the opportunity of exhibiting his constructions in steel wool, cardboard, bits of cloth etc.," only twelve justified the term *collage-découpage*. They are: 1. The Hat Makes the Man. 2. The Slightly Ill Horse. 3. The Swan is Quite Peaceable. 4. Disrobed. 5. The Song of the Flesh. 6. Aerography. 7. Massacre of the Innocents. 8. Little Piece for Eight Hands. 9. Chinese Nightingale. 10. Ingres Gas-metric. 11. Switzerland, Birthplace of Dada. 12. The Steamer and the Fish.

As for the forty-four others, Aragon placed them in saying that "the place to catch hold of the thought of Max Ernst is where with a bit of color, some crayon, he attempts to acclimate the phantom which he is about to plunge into a strange landscape."[7]

He was right, because it was at this point that the bright bridge was flung between those two procedures which prompted the inspiration; *frottage* and *collage*. The similarity of the two is such that I can, without changing many words, use the terms employed earlier for the one, to relate how I made the discovery of the other.

One rainy day in 1919, finding myself in a village on the Rhine, I was struck by the obsession which held under my gaze the pages of an illustrated catalogue showing objects designed for anthropologic, microscopic, psychologic, mineralogic, and paleontologic demonstration. There I found brought together elements of figuration so remote that the sheer absurdity of that collection provoked a sudden intensification of the visionary faculties in me and brought forth an illusive succession of contradictory images, double, triple and multiple images, piling up on each other with the persistence and rapidity which are peculiar to love memories and visions of half-sleep.

These visions called themselves new planes, because of their meeting in a new unknown (the plane of non-agreement). It was enough at that time to embellish these catalogue pages, in painting or drawing, and thereby in gently reproducing only that which *saw itself in me*, a color, a pencil mark, a landscape foreign to the represented objects, the desert, a tempest, a geological cross-section, a floor, a single straight line signifying the horizon. . . . thus I obtained a faithful fixed image of my hallucination and transformed into revealing dramas my most secret desires — from what had been before only some banal pages of advertising.

Under the title "La Mise sous Whisky-Marin" I assembled and exhibited in Paris (May 1920) the first results obtained by this procedure, from the *Phallustrade* to *The Wet Nurse of the Stars*.

7. Aragon. *A Challenge to Painting.*

14

What are the collages of Max Ernst of which every child
worthy of the name should know the nomenclature by heart?

The phallustrade. The vernal robe of the muse. The shadow of a great dada.[8] Unheard-of menace, coming from one knows not where. Bone-mill of the peaceable hairdressers. All the transverse and longitudinal cross-sections. Sagging relief, taken from the lungs of a 47-year-old smoker. The acerbity of the mattress.

The preparation of the bone-glue. Hypertrophic trophy. Do not smile. Religious dada. Ambiguous figure.

The little tear duct that says tic-tac.

The hat makes the man.

When half grown the women are carefully poisoned — they are preserved in bottles — the little American girl whom we bring out this year amuses herself by suckling the dogs of the sea. — the human eye is embroidered with Rupert's drops of curdled air and salted snow (Knitted relief).

The canalization of gas. The galactometric forehead. The ascaride of sand. The guardian angel. Dehumanized seed. Three figures without sex. The stamens of Arp. Half-world of the two worlds.

The transfiguration of the chameleon on Mount Tabor is made in an elegant limousine while the angels and canaries fly away from the houses of man and while the very holy robe of Our Lord cries out de profundis *three times before whipping the flesh of the exhibitionists.*

Somnambulist elevator.

Opulent Mimi of love. The little Venus of the Eskimos.

Gay awakening of the geyser. Young man burdened with a faggot. Guardhouse drums of the celestial army. Childhood learns dada. Charity and voluptuousness.

The bed-chamber of Max Ernst.

The Chinese nightingale. The seed of the pyramids.

The dog who spits. The dog, well-coiffured in spite of the difficulties of the terrain, caused by an abundant snowfall. The woman with the beautiful throat . . . the song of the flesh.

Dada Degas. Dada Gauguin. The volume of the man, calculable by the accessories of the woman.

Wet-nurse of the stars.

It is now the twenty-second time that Lohengrin has abandoned his fiancee (for the first time) . . . and the earth has stretched her bark over four violins. We shall never meet again . . . we shall never give battle to the angels. . . . The swan is so peaceful . . . he rows furiously to reach Leda.

8. Do not forget, we are in 1919.

15

The orthochromatic Ferris-wheel. *Erectio sine qua non*. Ask your doctor. Here, everything is floating. . . .

Little machine built by minimax dadamax in person, serving to salt without fear the female sucking-cups at the beginning of the critical age.

Above the clouds walks the midnight. Above the midnight the invisible bird of day looks down. A little higher than the bird the air moves, and the walls and the roofs float.

Landscape in old iron: error of those who prefer navigating on the grass to a bust of a woman.

What is a Phallustrade?

It is an alchemic product, composed of the following elements: the auto-strade, the balustrade and a certain quantity of phallus. A phallustrade is a verbal collage. One might define collage as an alchemy resulting from the unexpected meeting of two or more heterogeneous elements, those elements provoked either by a will which — from a love of clairvoyance — is directed toward systematical confusion and disorder of all the senses (Rimbaud), or by hazard, or by a will favorable to hazard.[9] Hazard, as Hume defined it, is: *the equivalent of ignorance in which we find ourselves in relation to the real causes of events*, a definition which is increasingly corroborated by the development of calculations regarding probabilities, and by the importance which this dis-cipline holds in modern sciences and practical life: microphysics, astrophysics, biology, agronomy, demography, etc.[10]

Hazard is also — and this very difficult aspect of hazard has been neglected by the seekers of the "laws of chance" — *the master of humor* and conse-quently, in an epoch which is far from rosy (the epoch in which we live), in which a beautiful act consists in losing one's two arms in combat with his fellow men, the master of the humor-that-isn't-rosy, the *black humor*.

A phallustrade is a typical product of black humor. A sagging relief, taken from the lung of a 47-year-old smoker, is another. It has been said that the pre-dominant note in my collages of the dada period is this humor. But this is not

9. In the hope of increasing the fortuity of the elements entering the composition of a drawing and thus augment the suddenness of associations, the surrealists had recourse to a procedure which they called "Ex-quisite Corpse," and which consists in making a drawing of a person by several people. The paper is folded and each collaborator draws his part, without knowing what form the drawing has so far taken.

The considerable part played by hazard is limited here only by a kind of mental contagion. To judge by the results, we find the procedure able to produce strong, pure surrealist images. As Breton says: "For me, the strongest surrealist image is that which represents the highest degree of arbitrariness, that which one has the hardest time to translate into a practical language, whether it conceals an enormous amount of apparent contradiction, or one of its terms is curiously hidden, or, in announcing itself sensational, it comes untied feebly (so that it closes suddenly the angle of its compass), or it justifies itself in a formally derisive manner, or it is hallucinatory, or it very naturally lends the mask of the concrete to the abstract or vice-versa, or it involves the negation of some elementary physical quality, or it provokes laughter. (*Surrealist Manifesto*).

10. Arp, in certain of his works, is guided by the "laws of hazard."

always so and in certain of these collages humor doesn't appear at all. (The Somnambulist Elevator, The Massacre of the Innocents, Above the Clouds. . . .) It seems to me one can say that collage is a hypersensitive and rigorously true instrument, like a seismograph, capable of registering the exact quantity of possibilities for human happiness in each epoch. The quantity of black humor contained in each authentic collage is found there in the inverse proportion of the possibilities for happiness (objective and subjective).

This invalidates the opinion of those who wish to see, in the pretended absence of all humor in surrealist painting, the essential difference between surrealist and dadaist works: can they believe that our epoch is any rosier than the years 1917–1921?

What is the most noble conquest of collage?

The irrational. The magisterial eruption of the irrational in all domains of art, of poetry, of science, in the private life of individuals, in the public life of peoples. He who speaks of collage speaks of the irrational. Collage has crept slyly into our common objects. We have acclaimed its appearance in the surrealist films (I am thinking of *The Golden Age* of Bunuel and Dali: the cow in the bed, the bishop and the giraffe flung through the window, the chariot crossing the salon of the governor, the Minister of the Interior glued to the ceiling after his suicide, etc.). In assembling collages one after another, without choice, we have been surprised by the clarity of the irrational action that resulted: *The Hundred-Headed Woman* (*Woman Without a Head*), the *Dream of a Little Girl Who Wished to Enter Carmel*, the *Week of Kindness*. Do not forget this other conquest of collage: *surrealist painting*, in at least one of its multiple aspects, that which, between 1921 and 1924, I was the only one to develop[11] and in which, later, while I advanced alone, feeling my way, into the yet unexplored forests of *frottage*, others continued their researches (Magritte, for example, whose pictures are collages entirely painted by hand, and Dali).

When the thoughts of two or more authors were systematically fused into a single work (otherwise called collaboration) this fusion could be considered as akin to collage. I quote as examples two texts resulting from the collaboration of my good friend Paul Eluard and myself; the first taken from *Misfortunes of the Immortals* (1922), the second from an unfinished book which proposed to find new techniques in the practice of love, *Et Suivant Votre Cas* (1923).

11. Chirico, to whom I pay homage in passing, had already taken another road, as we know.
Everyone knows the other extremely important aspects of surrealist painting of which the most authentic representatives are Arp, Tanguy, Miro, Man Ray, Picasso and Giacometti, and which began with the *papier collés* of Braque and Picasso.

17

Shattered fans

The crocodiles of today are no longer crocodiles. Where are the good old adventurers who caught you in the nostrils of miniscule bicycles and pretty ear-drops of ice? Following the speed of the finger, the racers at the four cardinal points paid each other compliments. What a pleasure it was then to lean with graceful abandon upon those agreeable rivers salted with pigeons and pepper!

There are no more real birds. In the evening the taut cords on the way home did not trip anyone, but at each false obstacle smiles cut a little deeper into the eyes of the acrobats. The dust smelled of the thunderbolt. Formerly, the good old fish wore beautiful red shoes on their fins.

There are no more real water-bicycles, nor microscopy, nor bacteriology. On my word, the crocodiles of today are no longer crocodiles.

Series of Young Women

The woman lying on a flat surface, a table for example, is covered by a cover folded in half.

One presents the object to her by placing it above her head and within the radius of her vision. Lower the object slowly, so that the woman follows it with her gaze, then raises her head, and bends her neck, the chin coming in contact with the breast.

Remain thus a moment, then return gently to the starting position. It is preferable that the object be shiny and of a lively color.

Seat the woman on the table, letting her arrange her arms and legs as she likes.

Attract her attention with the object placed above her head, move it, lower it toward the right, continue the movement downward then bring it up again toward the left. Always hold the object far enough away that the woman cannot grasp it. Abandon it to her only to reward her for her efforts.

III. *Instantaneous Identity*

If one is to believe the description of Max Ernst contained in his identity papers he would be only 45 years old at the moment of writing these lines. He would have an oval face, blue eyes and pale hair. His height would not be over average — or under, either. As for any particular marks the identity papers accord him none. Consequently he could, if pursued by the police, easily plunge into the crowd and disappear forever. The women, however, find his face young and framed with silky white hair which "makes him look distinguished." They credit him with charm, a great deal of "reality" and seduction, a perfect physique and agreeable manners (the danger of pollution, according to his own confession, has become such an old habit with him that he is proudly pleased with it as a sign of urbanity) but a difficult character, hopelessly complex, obstinate and with an impenetrable mind ("he is a nest of contradictions," they say) transparent and full of enigma at the same time.

It is hard for them to reconcile the gentleness and moderation of his expressions with the calm violence which is the essence of his thought. They readily compare him to a very light earthquake which gently displaces the furniture yet is in no hurry to change the position of things. What they find particularly disagreeable, even insupportable, is their almost total lack of success in discovering his IDENTITY in the flagrant contradictions (apparent) which exist between his spontaneous comportment and the dictates of his conscious thought. Regarding "nature" for example, one may discern in him two attitudes, in appearance irreconcilable: that of the god Pan and the man Papou who possesses all the mysteries and realizes the playful pleasure in his union with her ("He marries nature, he pursues the nymph Echo," they say) and that of a conscious and organized Prometheus, thief of fire who, guided by thought, persecutes her with an implacable hatred and grossly injures her. "This monster is pleased only by the antipodes of the landscape," they repeat. And a teasing little girl adds: "He is a brain and a vegetable at the same time."

Nevertheless, these two attitudes (contradictory in appearance but in reality simply in a state of conflict) that he displays in nearly every domain are convulsively fused into one each time he comes face to face with a fact (such as a tree, a stone, an eye, etc.) and this union is brought about in the same way as that other: when one brings two distant realities together on an apparently antipathetic plane (that which in simple language is called "collage") an exchange of energy transpires, provoked by this very meeting. This exchange, which might be a broad flowing stream or a shattering stroke of lightning and thunder, I am tempted to consider the equivalent of that which, in classical philosophy, is called *identity*. I conclude, in transposing the thought of André Breton, that IDENTITY WILL BE CONVULSIVE OR WILL NOT EXIST.

Translated by Dorothea Tanning.

Inspiration to Order

(This text served later as the sketch on which the more complete "Beyond Painting" was based.)

Since the becoming of no work which can be called absolutely surrealist is to be directed consciously by the mind (whether through reason, taste, or the will), the active share of him hitherto described as the work's "author" is suddenly abolished almost completely. This "author" is disclosed as being a mere spectator of the birth of the work, for, either indifferently or in the greatest excitement, he merely watches it undergo the successive phases of its development. Just as the poet has to write down what is being thought — voiced — inside him, so the painter has to limn and give objective form to *what is visible inside him.*

Upon the publication of André Breton's *Manifesto of Surrealism*, sceptics and humorists alike asserted that to produce works in this way could only be within the power of mediums, visionaries, and in general those endowed with second sight. "Everybody now knows that there is no *surrealist painting.* Neither the pencil lines drawn by chance movements, nor the pictures reproducing dream images, nor imaginative fancies, can of course be so described." It was in this strain that in number three of *La Révolution Surréaliste* (April 1925) one of the editors, M. Pierre Naville, sought to discourage us. Yet at the very time he was thus prophesying, the "unconscious" had, as one could easily establish, already made a dramatic appearance in the practical realm of painted and drawn poetry.

Thanks to studying enthusiastically the mechanism of inspiration, the surrealists have succeeded in discovering certain essentially poetic processes whereby the plastic work's elaboration can be freed from the sway of the so-called conscious faculties. Amounting to a bewitching of either reason, taste, or the will, these processes result in the surrealist definition being rigorously applied to drawing, painting, and even to some extent photography; and although some of them — *collage*,[12] for instance — were being used before our advent, surrealism has so systematized and modified them that it is now possible to photograph either on paper or on canvas the amazing graphic appearances of thoughts and desires.

Being called upon to give here some idea of the first process to reveal itself to us and to put us on the track of others, I am inclined to say that it amounts to the exploiting of *the fortuitous encounter upon a non-suitable plane of two mutually distant realities* (this being a paraphrase and generalization of the celebrated Lautréamont quotation, "Beautiful as the chance meeting upon a dissecting table of a sewing-machine with an umbrella") or, to use a more handy expression, the cultivation of the effects of a *systematic putting out of place*, on the lines of André Breton's theory which he expounds as follows:

> Super-reality must in any case be a function of our will to put everything completely out of place (and of course (*a*) one may go so far as to put a hand out of place by isolating it from an arm, (*b*) the hand gains thereby *qua* hand, and (*c*) in speaking of putting out of place we are not referring merely to the possibility of action in space). ("Warning to the Reader" in *The Hundred-Headed Woman.*)

The way in which this process is most commonly carried out has led to its being currently described as *collage*.

Thanks to using, modifying and incidentally systematizing this process, nearly all the surrealists, painters as well as poets, have since its discovery been led from surprise to surprise. Among the finest results they have been fortunate enough to obtain, one must mention the creation of what they have called *surrealist objects*.

Let a ready-made reality with a naïve purpose apparently settled once for all (i.e. an umbrella) be suddenly juxtaposed to another very distant and no less ridiculous reality (i.e. a sewing-machine) in a place where both must be felt as *out of place* (i.e. upon a dissecting table), and precisely thereby it will be robbed of its naïve purpose and its identity; through a relativity it will pass from its false to a novel absoluteness, at once true and poetic: umbrella and sewing-machine will make love. This very simple example seems to me to reveal the mechanism of the process. Complete transmutation followed by a pure act such as the act of love must necessarily occur every time the given facts

---

12. The cutting-up of various flat reproductions of objects or of parts of objects and the pasting of them together to form a picture of something new and odd.

make conditions favourable : *the pairing of two realities which apparently cannot be paired on a plane apparently not suited to them.* Speaking in 1921 of the *collage* process, Breton wrote:

> It is the wonderful power to grasp two mutually distant realities without going beyond the field of our experience and to draw a spark from their juxtaposition; to bring within reach of our senses abstract forms capable of the same intensity and distinctness as others; and, while depriving us of any system of reference, to put us out of place in our very recollection — this is what, at the moment, he is concerned with. (Preface to the Max Ernst Exhibition of May, 1921.)

And he added prophetically: "May it not be that we are thus getting ready to break loose some day from the law of identity?"

An analogous mechanism to that of *collage* can be detected by the reader in the imposing image contained in the following proposal by Dali for a *surrealist object:*

> Let some huge motor-cars, three times as big as actual ones, be made in plaster or onyx with a thoroughness of detail greater than the most faithful moulds, let them be wrapped in women's underwear and buried in a graveyard, the spot being indicated merely by a thin yellow-coloured clock. (*Le Surréalisme au Service de la Révolution*, No. 3.)

In the hope of increasing the fortuitous character of elements utilizable in the composing of a drawing and so increasing their abruptness of association, surrealists have resorted to the process called "The Exquisite Corpse." The large share chance has in this is limited only by the role played for the first time by mental contagion. On the strength of the results obtained (see the reproductions in *La Révolution surréaliste*, Nos. 9 and 10, and in *Variétés* for June, 1929), we may consider that this process is particularly well suited for producing strong and pure surrealist images in accordance with the criteria laid down by Breton as follows:

> That, to my mind, [the surrealist image] is strong in proportion to the degree of arbitrariness it displays, I do not con-

ceal; I mean the image which it takes longest to describe in concrete words, either because it secretes an enormous amount of apparent contradiction, or because one of its terms is strangely lacking, or because while promising to be sensational it appears to unravel weakly (or closes the angle of its pair of compasses suddenly), or because it affords of itself only a ridiculous *formal* justification, or because it is of the hallucinatory kind, or because with the concrete it quite naturally only masks the abstract, or because inversely it would imply the negation of some elementary physical property, or because it is funny.

(*Manifesto of Surrealism.*)

In the days when we were most keen on research and most excited by our first discoveries in the realm of *collage*, we would come by chance, or as it seemed by chance, on (for example) the pages of a catalogue containing plates for anatomical or physical demonstration and found that these provided contiguously figurative elements so mutually distant that the very absurdity of their collection produced in us a hallucinating succession of contradictory images, super-imposed one upon another with the persistence and rapidity proper to amorous recollections. These images themselves brought forth a new plane in order to meet in a new unknown (the plane of non-suitability). Thereupon it was enough either by painting or by drawing to add, and thereby only obediently reproducing *what is visible within us,* a color, a scrawl, a landscape foreign to the objects depicted, the desert, the sky, a geological section, a floor, a single straight line expressing the horizon, and a fixed and faithful image was obtained; what previously had been merely a commonplace page of advertising became a drama revealing our most secret desires. To take another example, a Second Empire embellishment we had found in a manual of drawing came to display as we considered it a strong propensity to change into a chimera, which had about it something of bird and octopus and man and woman. Here we are seemingly already in touch with what Dali was later to call "the paranoiac image" or "multiple image." His words are as follows:

The way in which it has been possible to obtain a double image is clearly paranoiac. By a double image is meant such a representation of an object that it is also, without the slightest physical or anatomical change, the representation of another entirely different object, the second representation being equally devoid of any deformity or abnormality betraying arrangement.

Such a double image is obtained in virtue of the violence of the paranoiac thought which has cunningly and skilfully used the requisite quantity of pretexts, coincidences, etc., and so taken advantage of them as to exhibit the second image, which then replaces the dominant idea.

The double image (an example of which is the image of a horse which is at the same time the image of a woman) may be extended, continuing the paranoiac advance, and then the presence of another dominant idea is enough to make a third image appear (for example, the image of a lion), and so on, until there is a number of images limited only by the mind's degree of paranoiac capacity. (*Le Surréalisme au Service de la Révolution*, No. 1.)

May it not be that in this way we have already broken loose from the law of identity?

It remains to speak of another process in resorting to which I have been brought under the direct influence of the information concerning the mechanism of inspiration that is provided in the *Manifesto of Surrealism*. This process rests on nothing other than the *intensification of the mind's powers of irritability*, and in view of its technical features I have dubbed it *frottage* (rubbing), and it has had in my own personal development an even larger share than *collage*, from which indeed I do not believe it differs *fundamentally*.

Being one rainy day in an inn at the seaside, I found myself recalling how in childhood an imitation mahogany panel opposite my bed had served as optical excitant of a somnolence vision, and I was struck by the obsession now being imposed on my irritated gaze by the floor, the cracks of which had been deepened by countless scrubbings. I thereupon decided to examine the symbolism of this obsession and, to assist my meditative and hallucinatory powers, I obtained from the floor-boards a series of drawings by dropping upon them anyhow pieces of paper I then rubbed with blacklead. I emphasize the fact that the drawings thus obtained steadily lose, thanks to a series of suggestions and transmutations occurring to one spontaneously — similarly to what takes place in the production of hypnagogical visions — the character of the material being studied — wood — and assume the aspect of unbelievably clear images of a nature probably able to reveal the first cause of the obsession or to produce a simulacrum thereof. My curiosity being thus aroused and marvelling, I was led to examine in the same way, but indiscriminately, many kinds of material happening to be in my field of vision — leaves and their veins, the unravelled edges of sackcloth, the palette-knife markings on a "modern" picture, thread unrolled from its spool, etc., I have put together under the title of *Natural History* the first fruits of the *frottage* process from *Sea and Rain* to *Eve, the Only One Remaining to Us*. Later on, it was thanks to restricting my own active participation ever more and more, so as thereby to increase the active share of the powers of the mind, that I succeeded in looking on *like a spectator* at the birth of pictures such as: *Women Shouting as They Ford a River, Vision Provoked by the Words: "The Immovable Father," Man Walking on the Water, Taking a Girl by the Hand and Shoving Past Another; Vision Provoked by a Sheet of Blotting-Paper*, etc.

At first it seemed as if the *frottage* process could be used only for drawing. If one takes into consideration that it has since been successfully adapted to the technical media of painting (scratching of pigments on a ground prepared in colors and placed over an uneven surface, etc.) without the slightest liberty being taken with the principle of the intensification of the mind's powers of irritability, I think I am entitled to say without exaggeration that surrealism has enabled painting to travel with seven-league boots a long way from Renoir's three apples, Manet's four sticks of asparagus, Derain's little chocolate women, and the Cubists' tobacco-packet, and to open up for it a field of *vision* limited only by the *irritability capacity of the mind's powers*. Needless to say, this has been a great blow to art critics, who are terrified to see the importance of the "author" being reduced to a minimum and the conception of "talent" abolished. Against them, however, we maintain that surrealist painting is within the reach of everybody who is attracted by real revelations and is therefore ready to assist inspiration or make it work to order.

We do not doubt that in yielding quite naturally to the vocation of pushing back appearances and upsetting the relations of "realities," it is helping, with a smile on its lips, to hasten the general crisis of consciousness due in our time.

Some Data on the Youth of M.E. *as told by himself*

The 2nd of April (1891) at 9:45 a.m. Max Ernst had his first contact with the sensible world, when he came out of the egg which his mother had laid in an eagle's nest and which the bird had brooded for seven years. It happened in Brühl, 6 miles south of Cologne. Max grew up there and became a beautiful child. His childhood is marked by some dramatic incidents, but was not particularly unhappy.

Cologne was a former Roman colony called *Colonia Claudia Agrippina* and later the most radiant medieval culture-center of the Rhineland. It is still haunted by the splendid magician Cornelius Agrippa who was born there and by Albert the Great who worked and died in this town. The craniums and bones of three other magi: Jasper, Melchior and Balthasar, the wise men of the East, are preserved in the dome-cathedral. Every year, the 6th of January, their golden, sumptuously jeweled coffin is shown to the public with extraordinary pagan pomp. Eleven thousand virgins gave up their lives in Cologne rather than give up chastity. Their gracious skulls and bones embellish the walls of the convent-church in Brühl, the same one where little Max was forced to pass the most boring hours of his childhood. Maybe their company was helpful to him.

Cologne is situated just on the border of a wine-producing region. North of Cologne is Beerland, south is wineland (Rhineland). Are we what we drink? If so it may be important to state that Max always preferred wine. When he was two years old, he secretly emptied some glasses, then he took his father by the hand, showed him the trees in the garden and said, "Look, daddy, they move." When later he learned the story of the Thirty Years' War (1618–1648), he had the impression that this was a war of beer drinkers against wine drinkers. Perhaps he was right.

The geographical, political and climatic conditions of Cologne may be propitious to create fertile conflicts in a sensible child's brain. There is the cross-point of the most important European culture-tendencies, early Mediterranean influence, western rationalism, eastern inclination to occultism, northern mythology, Prussian categorical imperative, ideals of the French Revolution and so on. In Max Ernst's work one can recognize a continuous powerful drama of those contradictory tendencies. Maybe one day some elements of a new mythology will spring out of this drama.

Little Max's first contact with painting occurred in 1894 when he saw his father at work on a small water color entitled "Solitude" which represented a hermit sitting in a beech-forest and reading a book. There was a terrifying, quiet atmosphere in this "Solitude" and in the manner it was treated. Everyone of the thousand of beech-leaves was scrupulously and minutely executed, everyone of them had its individual solitary life. The monk was terrifically absorbed by the content of his book, so that he represented something living outside the world. Even the sound of the word "Hermit" exercised a shuddering magic power on the child's mind. (The same thing happened to him at this time by the sound of the words "Charcoal-Monk-Peter" and "Rumpelstilzkin.") Max never forgot the enchantment and terror he felt, when a few days later his father conducted him for the first time into the forest. One may find the echo of this feeling in many of Max Ernst's *Forests and Jungles* (1925–1942).

(1896) Little Max made a series of drawings. They represented father, mother, the one-year-older sister Maria, himself, two younger sisters Emmy and Louise, a friend named Fritz and the railroad guardian, all of them standing, only the six-month-old Louise sitting (too young for standing). In the sky an abundantly smoking train. When someone asked him: "What will you become later?" little Max regularly answered: "A railroad guardian." Maybe he was seduced by the nostalgia provoked by passing trains and the great mystery of telegraphic wires which move when you look at them from a running train and stand still, when you stand still. To scrutinize the mystery of the telegraphic wires (and also to flee from the father's tyranny) five-year-old Max escaped from his parents' house. Blue-eyed, blond-curly-haired, dressed in a red night shirt, carrying a whip in the left hand, he walked in the middle of a pilgrims' procession. Enchanted by this charming child and believing it was the vision of an angel or even the infant of the virgin, the pilgrims proclaimed "Look, little Jesus Christ." After a mile or so little Jesus Christ escaped from the procession, directed himself to the station and had a long and delightful trip beside the railroad and the telegraphic wires.

To appease father's fury, when the next day a policeman brought him home, little Max proclaimed that he was sure he was little Jesus Christ. This candid remark inspired the father to make a portrait of his son as a little Jesus-child, blue-eyed, blond-curly-haired, dressed in a red night shirt, blessing the world with the right hand and bearing the cross — instead of the whip — in his left.

Little Max, slightly flattered by this image, had however some difficulty in throwing off the suspicion that daddy took secret pleasure in the idea of being God-the-Father, and that the hidden reason of this picture was a blasphemous pretension. Maybe Max Ernst's picture "Souvenir de Dieu" (1923) has a direct connection with the remembrance of this fact.

(1897) First contact with nothingness, when his sister Maria kissed him and her sisters goodbye and died a few hours afterwards. Since this event the feeling of nothingness and annihilating powers were predominant in his mind, in his behaviour and — later — in his work.

(1897) First contact with hallucination. Measles. Fear of death and the annihilating powers. A fever-vision provoked by an imitation-mahogany panel opposite his bed, the grooves of the wood taking successively the aspect of an eye, a nose, a bird's head, a *menacing nightingale*, a spinning top and so on. Certainly little Max took pleasure in being afraid of these visions and later delivered himself voluntarily to provoke hallucinations of the same kind in looking obstinately at wood-panels, clouds, wallpapers, unplastered walls and so on to let his "imagination" go. When someone would ask him: "What is your favorite occupation?" he regularly answered, "Looking."

An analogous obsession conducted Max Ernst later to search for and discover some technical possibilities of drawing and painting, directly connected with the processes of inspiration and revelation (*frottage, collage, decalcomania*, etc.) Possibly "Two Children Are Menaced by a Nightingale" (1924) was some connection with the fever-vision of 1897.

(1898) Second contact with painting. He saw his father make a painting *après nature* in the garden and finish it in his studio. Father suppressed a tree in his picture, because it disturbed the "composition." Then he suppressed the same tree in the garden so that there was no more difference between nature and art. The child felt a revolt growing in his heart against candid realism and decided to direct himself towards a more equitable conception of the relationship between the subjective and the objective world.

(1906) First contact with occult, magic and witchcraft powers. One of his best friends, a most intelligent and affectionate pink cockatoo, died in the night of January the 5th. It was an awful shock to Max when he found the corpse in the morning and when, at the same moment, his father announced to him the birth of sister Loni. The *perturbation* of the youth was so enormous that he fainted. In his imagination he connected both events and charged the baby with extinction of the bird's life. A series of mystical crises, fits of hysteria, exaltations and depressions followed. A dangerous confusion between birds and humans became encrusted in his mind and asserted itself in his drawings and paintings. The obsession haunted him until he erected the *Birds' Memorial Monument* in 1927, and even later Max identified himself voluntarily with *Loplop, the Superior of the Birds.* This phantom remained inseparable from another one called *Perturbation ma soeur, la femme 100 têtes.*

(1906–1914) Excursions in the world of marvels, chimeras, phantoms, poets, monsters, philosophers, birds, women, lunatics, magi, trees, eroticism, stones, insects, mountains, poisons, mathematics and so on. A book that he wrote at this time was never published. His father found and burned it. The title of the book was "Divers' Manual."

(1914) Max Ernst died the 1st of August 1914. He resuscitated the 11th of November 1918 as a young man aspiring to become a magician and to find the myth of his time. Now and then he consulted the eagle who had hatched the egg of his pre-natal life. You may find the bird's advices in his work.

(1941) The bird followed the plane which brought Max to this country on the 14th of July and built his nest in a cloud on the East River.

Max Ernst: *Paintings Collages Sculptures*

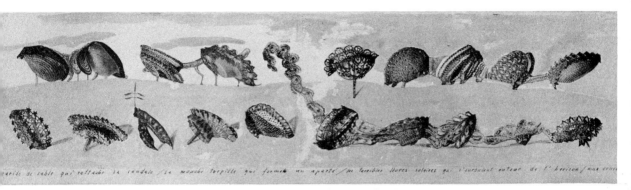

The Sandworm Attaches Its Sandal, *gouache, collage,* 1921

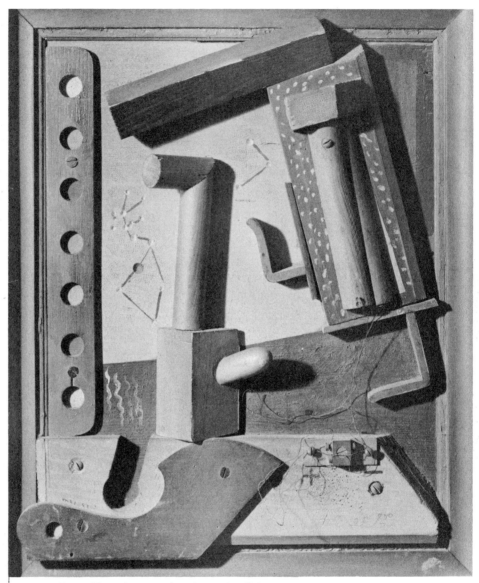

Fruit of a Long Experience, *painted wood relief*, 1919

Woman, Old Man and Flower, *oil*, 1924

Katharina Ondulata, *gouache on wallpaper*, 1920

Napoleon in the Wilderness, *oil*, 1941

Dada in Usum Delphini, *gouache, collage,* 1920

Right, Revolution by Night, *oil,* 1923

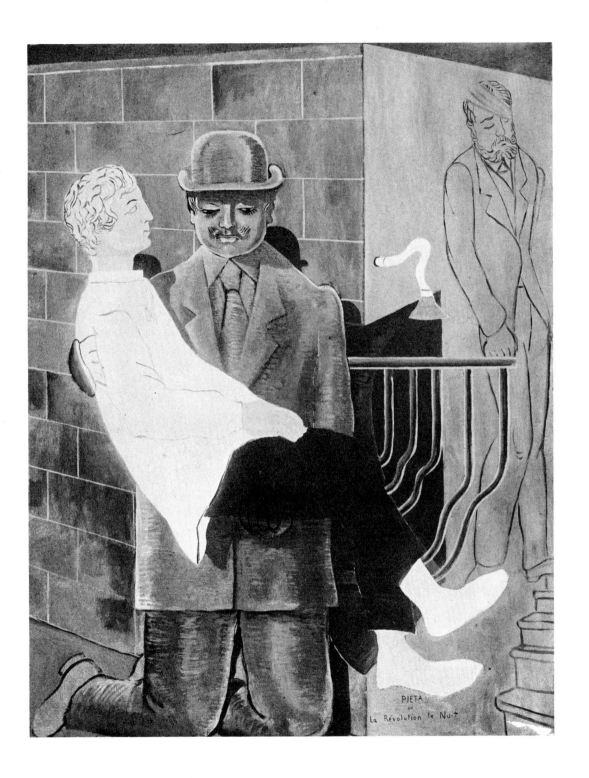

Still Death, *watercolor*, 1923

Loplop, *gouache, collage,* 1931

41

Winter Landscape, *gouache, collage,* 1921

The Bewildered Planet, *oil*, 1942

Sun and Forest, *oil*, 1926

Here Everything is Floating, *collage*, 1920

Birds, *gouache*, 1929

The Hundred Thousand Doves, *oil*, 1927

47

Painting for Young People, *oil*, 1943

Still Death, *oil*, 1925

Garden Airplane Trap, *oil*, 1934

Summer Night in Arizona, *oil*, 1943

Moon Over Wellfleet, *oil*, 1942

The Foolish Virgins, *oil*, 1947

Sun, Sea and Earthquake, *oil*, 1929

Swamp Angel, *oil*, 1940

La Joie de Vivre, *oil*, 1937

57

The Blind Swimmer, *oil*, 1934

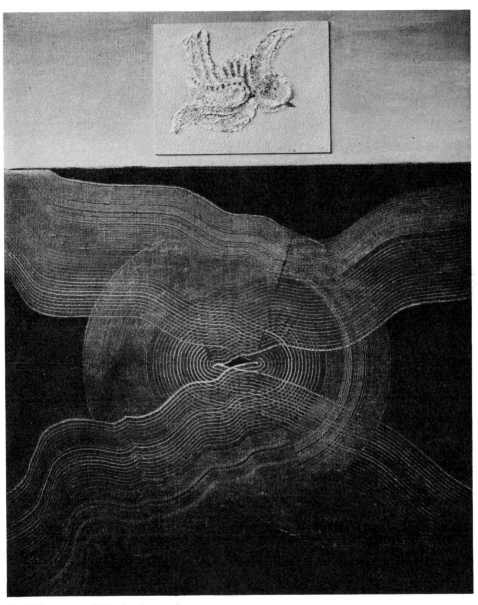

Gulf Stream and Bird, *oil*, 1926

Three Young Girls in Beautiful Poses, *oil*, 1927

Two Women and Monkey with Sticks, *oil*, 1927

Vision Provoked by the Words: the Immobile Father, *oil*, 1927

A Maiden's Dream about a Lake, *oil*, 1940

The Horde, *oil*, 1927

The Stolen Mirror, *oil*, 1940

Night of Love, *oil*, 1927

Shrieking Women Crossing a River, *oil*, 1927

Facility, *oil*, 1927

Mural Sculpture, *concrete*, 1938

Man and Bird, *oil on plaster*, 1930

Mural Sculpture, *concrete*, 1938

The Elephant of Celebes, *oil*, 1921

Sculpture, *concrete*, 1939

Demi-Mondes des Deux Mondes, *gouache on wallpaper*, 1920

Right, Gay, *plaster*, 1935

Birth of Comedy, *oil,* 1947

Moon Mad,   *mahogany*, 1944

Mural, 1939

The King Playing with the Queen, *plaster*, 1944

The Doves are Folded in Their Wings, *oil*, 1925   White Queen, *plaster*, 1944

81

Monument of the Birds, *oil*, 1927

Oedipus, *plaster*, 1934

Forest, *oil,* 1926

Lunar Asparagus,
plaster, 1934

85

Young Chimera in Evening Dress, *oil*, 1935

Chimeras, Snakes and Bottle, *plaster*, 1938

The Discovery of Gold, *oil*, 1947

An Anxious Friend, *plaster*, 1944

Flower, *oil*, 1928

Euclid, *oil*, 1945

91

The Blue Hour, *oil,* 1946/47

Cocktail Drinker, *oil,* 1945

The Dove was Right, *oil*, 1926

The Phases of the Night, *oil*, 1946

Flowers in a Landscape, *oil*, 1927

Le Déjeuner sur l'Herbre, *oil*, 1944

The Chinese Nightingale, *collage*, 1920

Gardenia, *oil*, 1945

Stage sets for "Ubu Enchainé," 1937

Low Relief, *granite*, 1934, *two views*

White Dove, Black Dove, *oil*, 1925

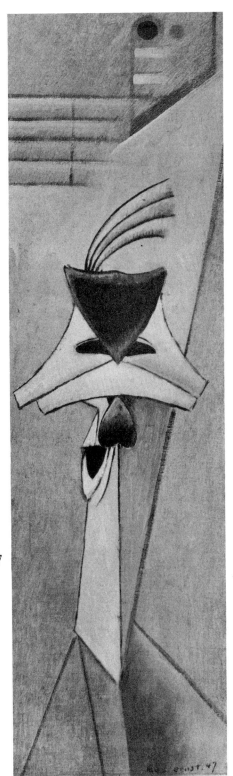

Head of a Woman, *oil*, 1947

Europe After the Rain, *oil*, 1940

Two Bishops fighting, *oil on paper*, 1934

Design in Nature, *oil*, 1947

The artist's studio, 1944

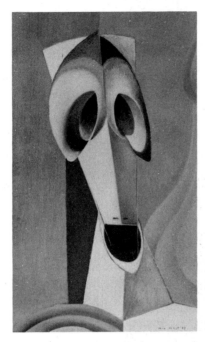

Head, *oil*, 1947

The artist's house, *France,* 1938

The Lent Ear, *oil*, 1935

Anthropomorphic Figure, 1928

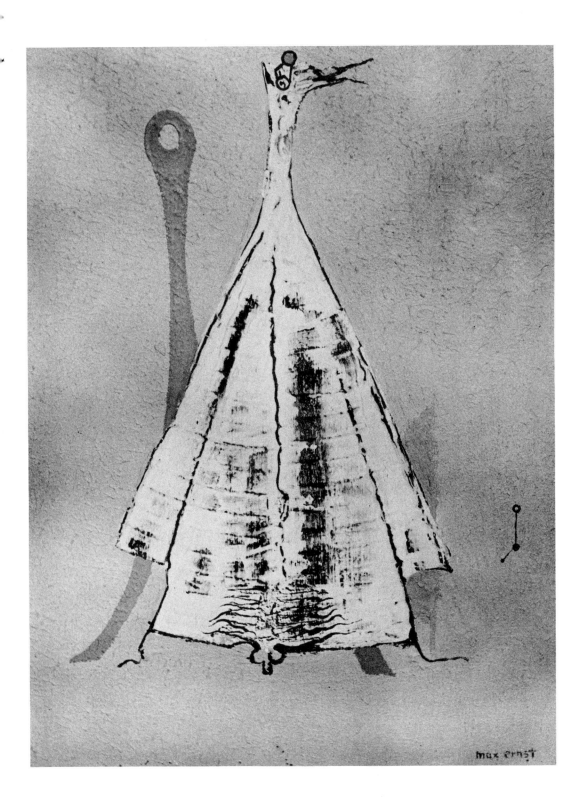

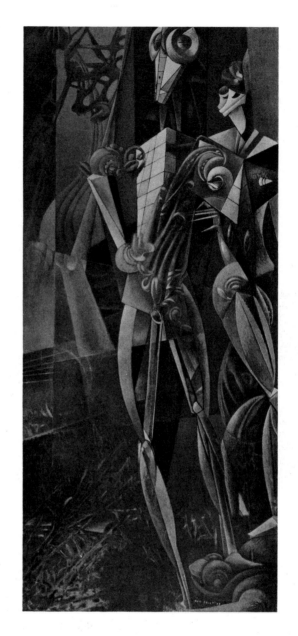

Chemical Nuptials, *oil*, 1948

Head of a young Girl, *oil*, 1948

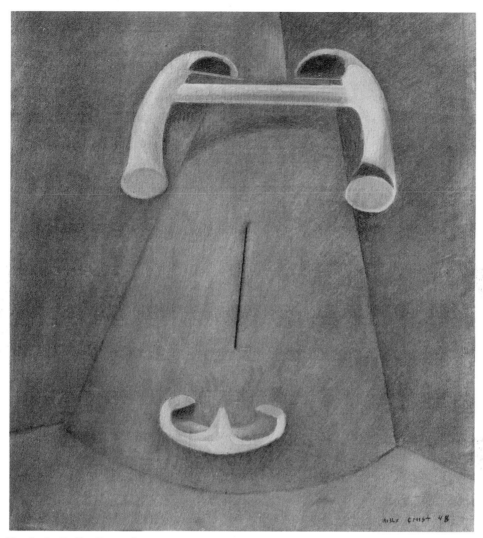

Head of a Bull, *oil*, 1948

Loplop Introduces a Young Girl, 1930

Capricorn, *concrete*, 8′ high, 1948 *and detail above*

Max Ernst: *Histoire Naturelle*

introduction to max ernst's natural history *by hans arp*

this introduction contains the pseudo-introduction the original the variants of the original the pseudo-original as well as the variants of the pseudo-original the apocrypha and the incorporation of all these texts in an original arpocryphum with apocopated whiskers as well as fifty calcinated medals and fifty suns of fifty years because the medal rises. — the medal of light rises. — fifty suns and fifty medals rise. — the wheels turn. — the wheels turn. — fifty suns and fifty medals rise while the pseudo-sun after fifty years of service retires into the calcinated wheels of light. — the wheels turn no more. — the wheels turn no more.

it is man who replaced alarm-clocks by earthquakes showers of jordan almonds by showers of hail. the shadow of man encountering the shadow of a fly causes a flood. thus it is man who has taught horses to embrace one another like presidents kings or emperors sucking each other's beards licking each other's snouts plunging their tongues into patriotic profundities. the passerby who sees these equine kisses thinks that peace has been established on earth forever.

with his eleven and a half tails of cotton his eight legs of bread his hundred eyes of air his four hearts of stone he goes a-hunting the flying cyclopean moustache without any limbs. but as this moustache is actually intelligible the hunter always comes home baffled. with the help of his eleven and a half tails man counts ten and a half objects in the furnished room of the universe: scarecrows with volcanoes and geysers in their buttonhole show cases of eruptions displays of lava string systems of solar currency labeled abdomens walls razed by poets the palettes of the caesars thoroughly still (and dead) lives the stables of the sphynxes the eyes of the man turned to stone while squinting at sodom the scars of . . .

enter the continents without knocking but with a muzzle of filigree

leaves never grow on the trees. like a mountain in bird's-eye view they have no perspective no soap no hybrid plastron no scotch cheeks no crypt. the spectator always finds himself in a false position before a leaf. he has the impression of carrying his head in his umbilicus his feet in his mouth his unwashed eyes in his hands. as for the branches trunks and roots I declare them to be fantasmagorias bald men's lies. branches trunks and roots do not exist.

like a lion who scents a succulent pair of newly-weds the seismic plant desires to make a meal of the dead man. in his millennial den made up as a foetus
it whirls with lust like the white juice of the end with the black juice of the
start and the ferocity of its gaze chases the navels around the earth. the lime-
tree grows tractably on boarded plains. the chestnut and the oak start out
under the banner of d.a.d.a. that is to say, domine anno domine anno. the cypress is not a dancer's calf in the ecclesiastical ballet.

while the ferocious lion scents a succulent pair of newly-weds the lime-
tree grows tractably on the boarded plains. when a traveler and a mountain
meet in the sky they become confounded with one another. the mountain takes
itself for the traveler and the traveler takes himself for the mountain. these
encounters always end in a bloody brawl in which the traveler and the mountain tear out each other's trees. the chestnut and the oak start out under the
sign of the vegetable banner. the cypress is a dancer's calf in an ecclesiastical
ballet.

the idol dreams in the sea and the rain. harnessed in fours ahead of the four
preceding like ventriloquists' cemeteries or fields of honor the insects emerge.

and now only eve remains to us. she is the white accomplice of newspaper
filchers. here is the cuckoo the origin of the clock. the sound of his jaws is like
the sound of a violent fall of hair. and so we count among the insects vaccinated bread the chorus of cells lightning flashes under fourteen years of age
and your humble servant.

the marine sky has been decorated by expressionist paperhangers who have
hung a shawl with frost-flowers on the zenith. in the season of the harvest of
conjugal diamonds huge cupboards with mirrors are found floating on their
back in the oceans. the mirrors of these cupboards are replaced by waxed
floors and the cupboard itself by a castle in spain. these mirrored cupboards
are rented as rings to midwives and storks to make their innumerable rounds
in and as tabourets to two gigantic rusty feet which rest upon them and sometimes tap a few steps *pam pam*. that is why the seas are called pampas because
pam means *pas* (step) and two *pas* make *pam pam*.

and so you see that one's honorable father can be consumed only slice by
slice. impossible to finish him in a single luncheon on the grass and even the
lemon falls on its knees before the beauty of nature.

The Sea and the Rain

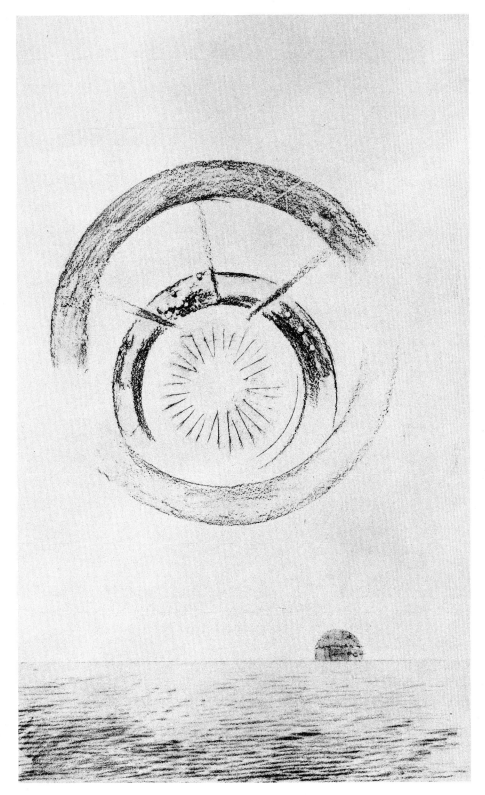

A Glance

Little Tables
around the Earth

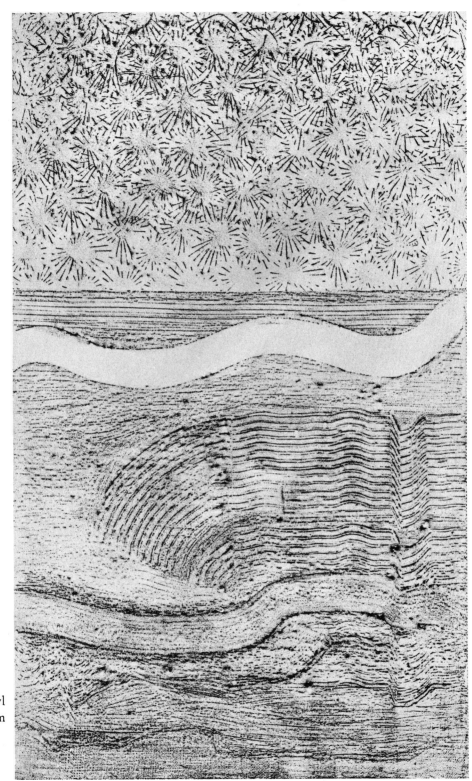

Iceflower Shawl
and Gulf Stream

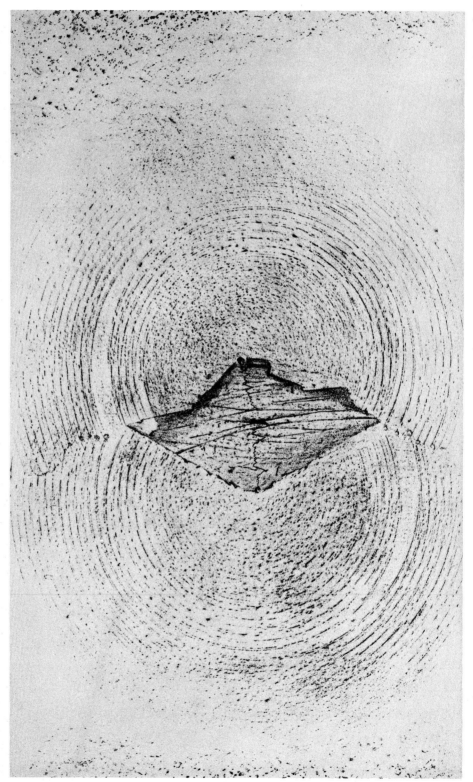

Earthquake

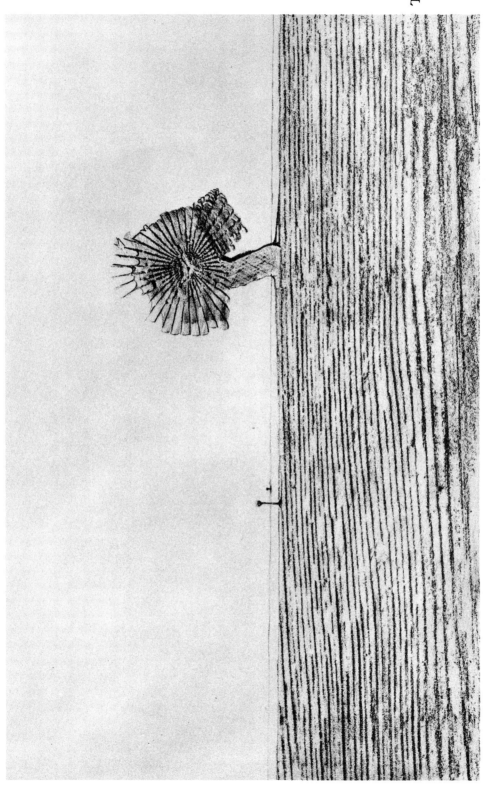

He Will Fall
Far from Here

132

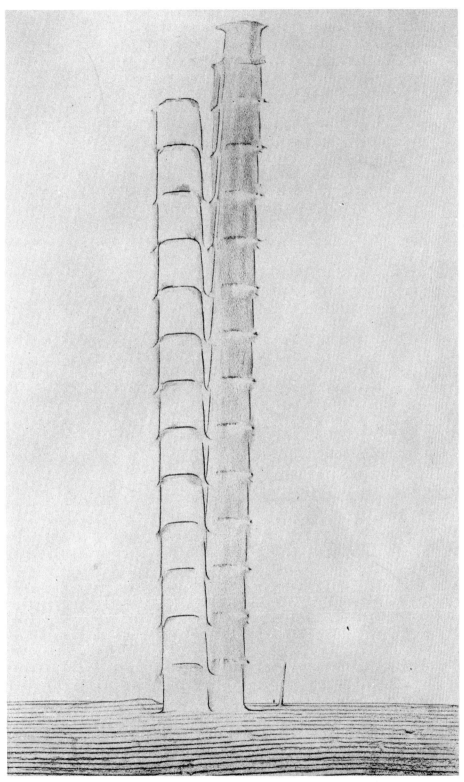

False Positions

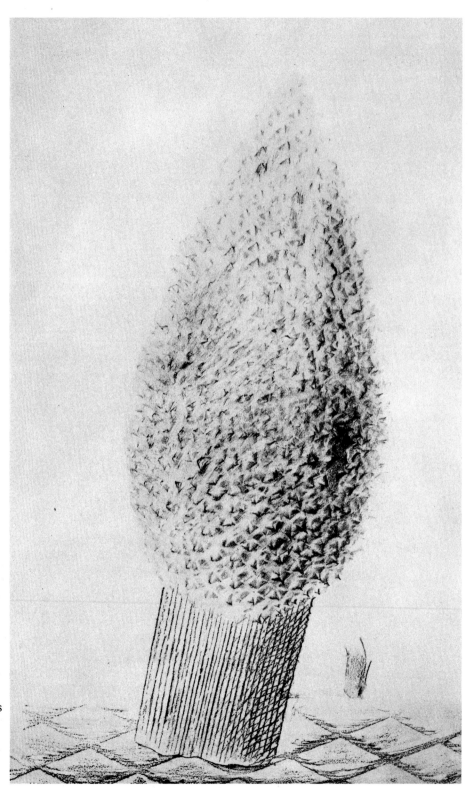

The Fascinating Cypress

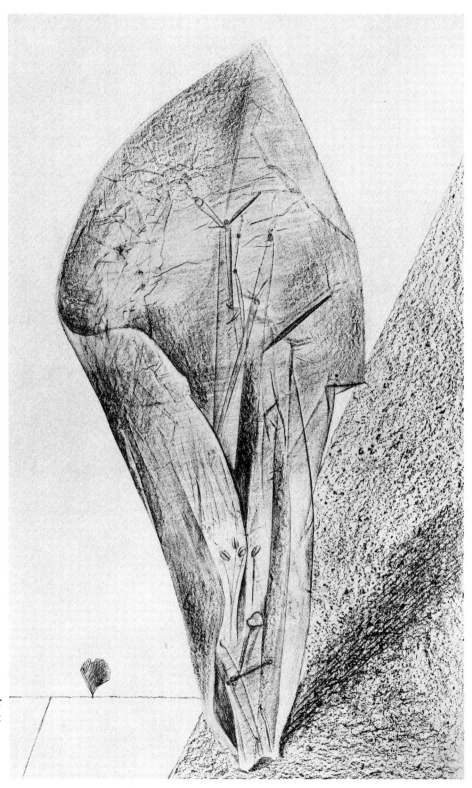

She Guards Her
Secret

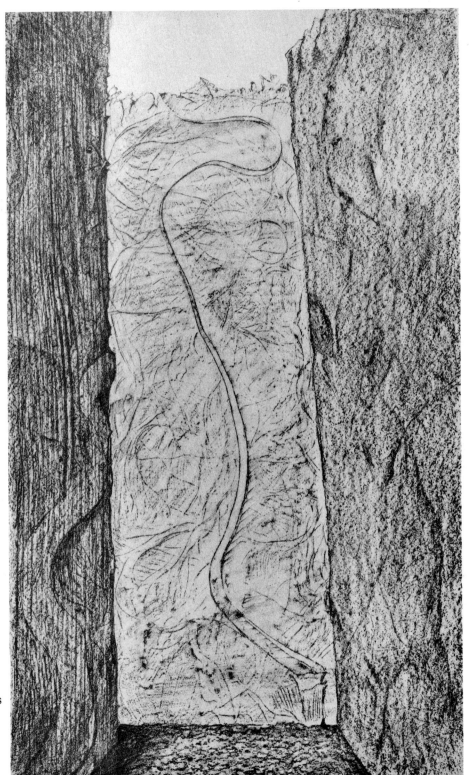

Scars

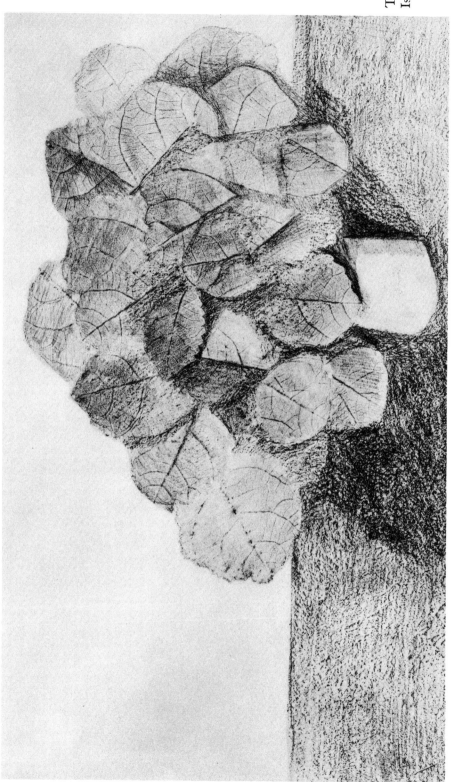

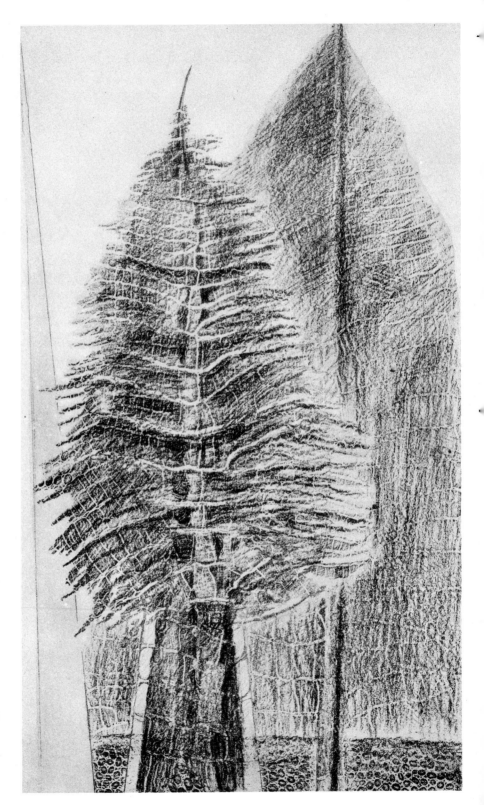

Confidences

142

Habits of Leaves

The Idol

Caesar's Palette

145

Shaving the Walls

146

Come into
the Continents

147

The Vaccinated Bread

n-Age Lightning

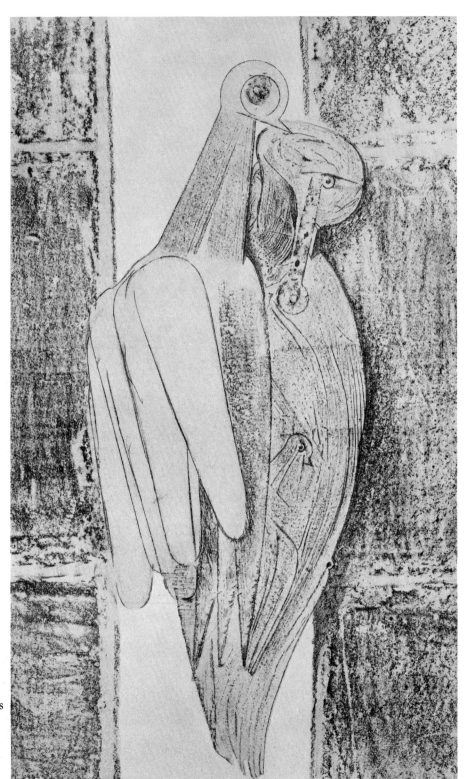

The Conjugal Diamonds

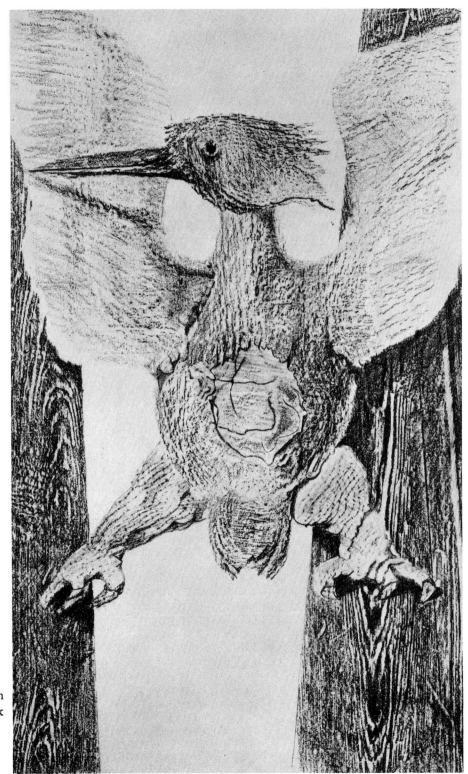

The Origin
of the Clock

151

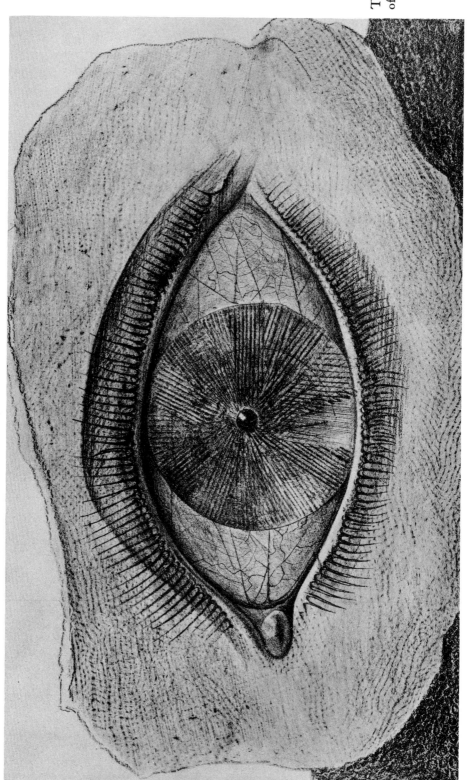

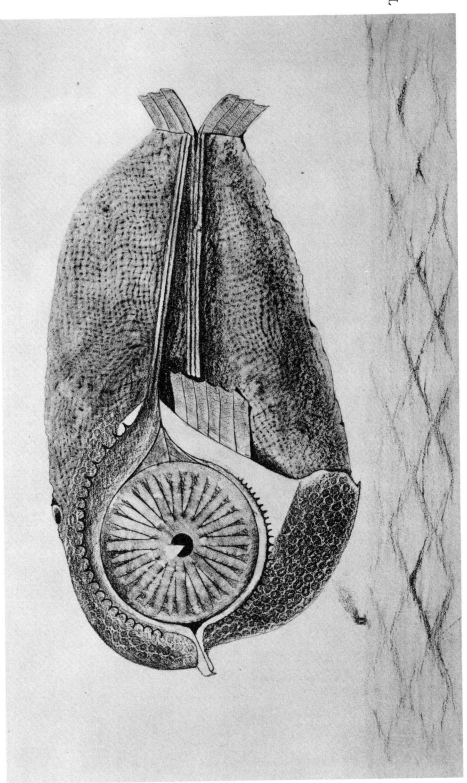

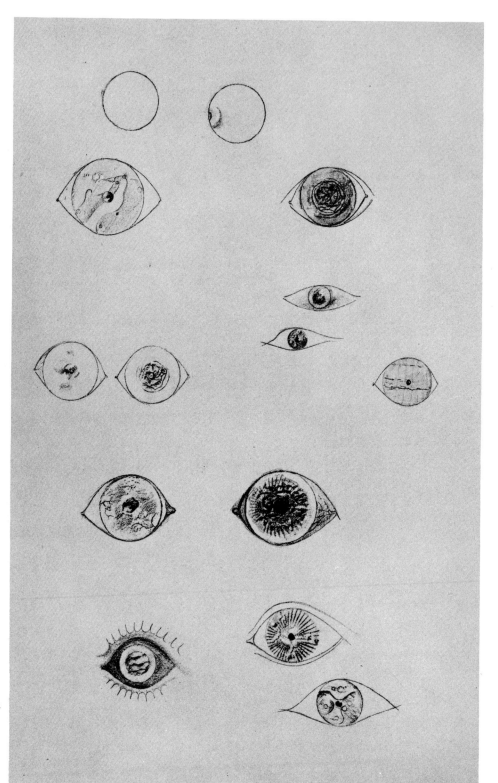

Solar Money-System

158

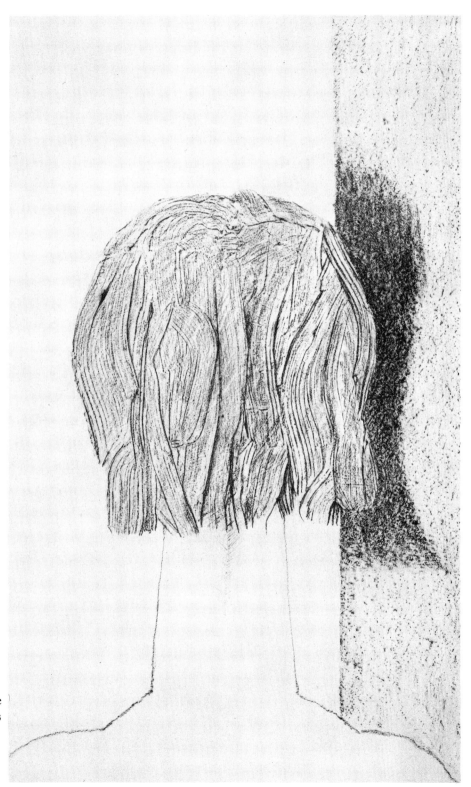

One day

from "*Une Semaine de Bonté*"

Paris, 1934

Element: Sight

Example: Inside of Sight

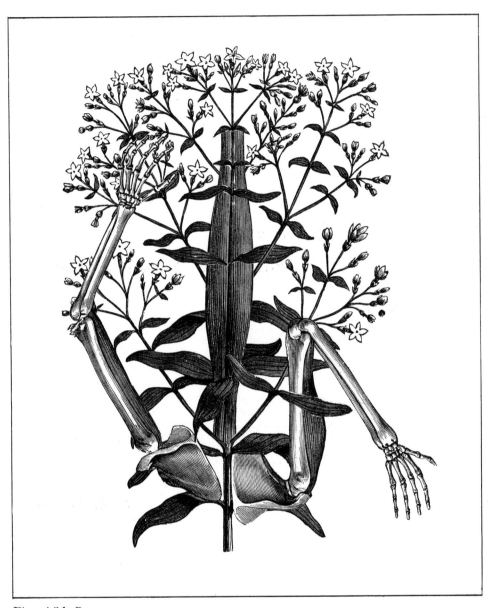

First visible Poem, no. 1

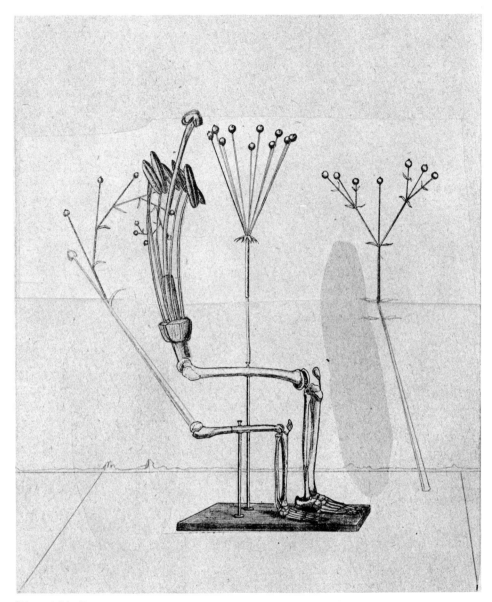

First visible Poem, no. 2

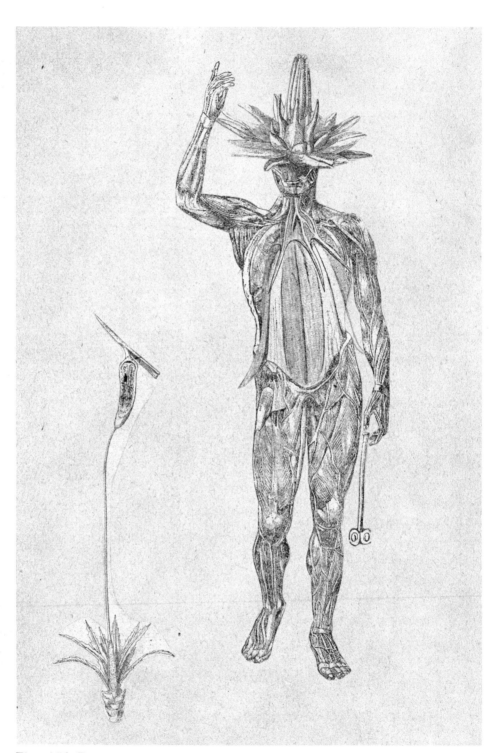

First visible Poem, no. 3

First visible Poem, no. 4

First visible Poem, no. 5

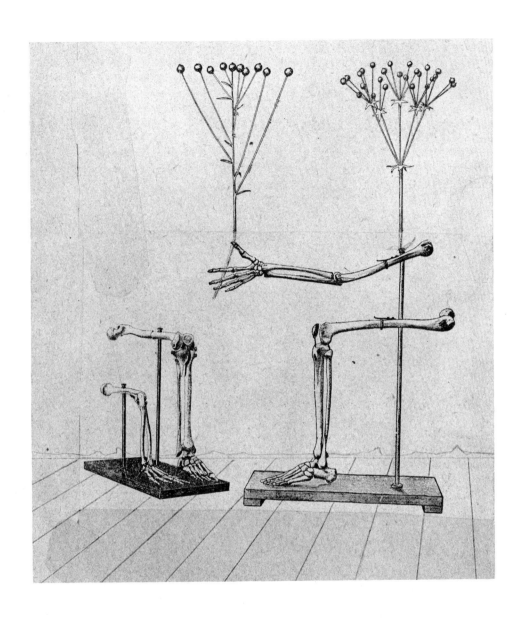

First visible Poem, no. 6

Second visible Poem, no. 1

Second visible Poem, no. 2

169

Second visible Poem, no. 3

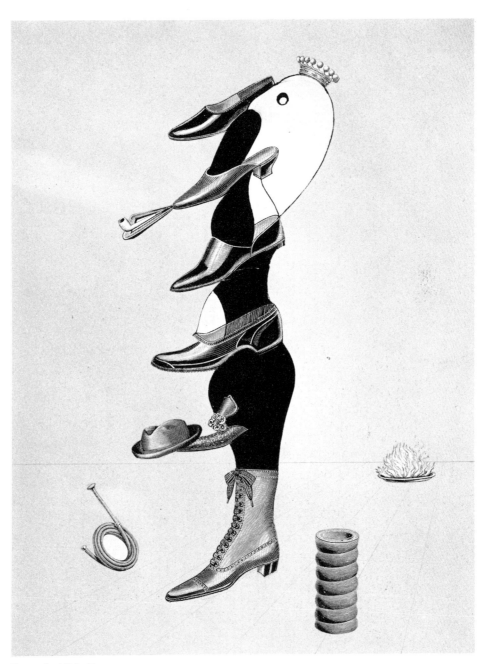

Second visible Poem, no. 4

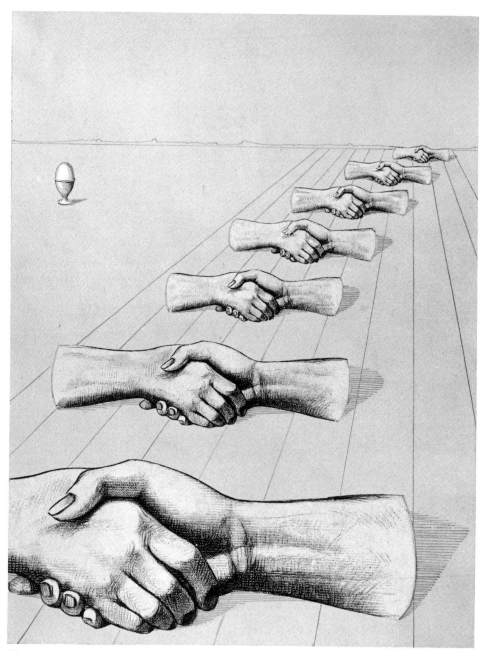

Third visible Poem, no. 1

Third visible Poem, no. 2

On Max Ernst: *by* *Breton*

Eluard

Ribemont-Dessaignes

Tzara

Levy

Calas

Matta

Max Ernst *by André Breton* (*1920*)

The invention of photography has dealt a mortal blow to the old modes of expression, in painting as well as in poetry, where automatic writing, which appeared at the end of the nineteenth century, is a true photography of thought. Since a blind instrument now assured artists of achieving the aim they had set themselves up to that time, they now aspired, not without recklessness, to break with the imitation of appearances. Unfortunately, human effort, which never ceases to vary the disposition of existing elements, cannot succeed in producing a single new element. A landscape into which nothing earthly enters is not within the reach of our imagination. And it seems likely that, denying *a priori* any effective value in such a landscape, we should refuse to evoke it. It would be equally sterile for us to reconsider the ready-made images of objects (as in catalogue figures) and the meanings of words, as though it were our mission to rejuvenate them. We must accept these conventions, and then we can distribute and group them according to whatever plan we please. It is because they failed to understand this essential freedom and its limitations that symbolism and futurism failed.

The belief in an absolute time and space seems to be vanishing. Dada does not pretend to be modern. It regards submission to the laws of any given perspective as useless. Its nature preserves it from attaching itself, even in the slightest degree, to matter, or from letting itself be intoxicated by words. It is the marvelous faculty of attaining two widely separate realities without departing from the realm of our experience, of bringing them together and drawing a spark from their contact; of gathering within reach of our senses abstract figures endowed with the same intensity, the same relief as other figures; and of disorienting us in our own memory by depriving us of a frame of reference — it is this faculty which for the present sustains Dada. Can such a gift not make the man whom it fills something better than a poet, since a poet is not obliged to have intelligence of his visions and since in any case he is compelled to maintain Platonic relations with them?

It still remains for us to consider certain rules similar to that of the three unities. Today, thanks to the cinema, we know how to make a locomotive *arrive* in a picture. As the use of slow motion and fast motion cameras becomes more general, as we grow accustomed to seeing oaks spring up and antelopes floating through the air, we begin to foresee with extreme emotion what this time-space of which people are talking may be. Soon the expression "as far as the eye can reach" will seem to us devoid of meaning, that is, we shall perceive the passage from birth to death without so much as blinking, and we shall observe infinitesimal variations. As it is easy to see by applying this method to the study of a boxing match, the only mechanism which it can possibly paralyze in us is that of suffering. Who knows whether we may not thus be preparing to escape one day from the principle of identity?

Because, in his determination to have done with the swindling mysticism of the still life, he projects before our eyes the most captivating film in the world and retains the grace to smile even while illuminating our interior life most profoundly and most radiantly, we do not hesitate to see in Max Ernst a man of these infinite possibilities.

177

Max Ernst *by André Breton* (*1927*)

I remember a very empty time (it was between 1919 and 1920) when all sorts of commonplace objects, intentionally thwarted in their meaning and application, rejected from the memory and as though traced over themselves, were ceaselessly born and ceaselessly died to several existences, when the word which hitherto had served to designate them no longer seemed adequate to them, when the properties that are ordinarily attributed to them were no longer in all evidence theirs, when a pessimistic desire for verification, which some will consider absurd, insisted on touching things that are sufficiently characterized by sight, and on perceiving the minutest details of what asks only to present itself as a totality, when the distinction between the necessary and the accidental had been lost. This was a profound disposition not only in me but in some others as well, and perhaps it is what led me to the point where I am. It was in the air, as everything is said to be in the air; functioning as a sign of this interior zodiac that I am unable to trace, it subjugated the most disparate minds. Derain, to cease quoting him, Derain for his present admirers would then have been hard to fathom. According to him, arithmetical addition and subtraction were meaningless. All nature, the tree for example in covering itself with leaves, knew no procedure other than multiplication. There would have been fifty other operations. Division worried him too: since to divide by any given number was always to divide by one (I have eaten ¾ of a duck. One thinks successively: I might have eaten ⅓, ⅔, but I ate the whole duck. Or, there were three people at table and I ate the

duck all by myself). Fashion and love had to be considered as games. According to Derain — and it would be hard to discern in these words what is innocence and what is cynicism — everything depended on adopting an attitude by which one was not duped, but which fatally duped others: the coitus considered as one of the most terrible dramas of the game (as soon as you see someone taking a similar attitude, you in turn are the dupe). The physical plane of objects was ill-defined; to say "the glass on the table" did not give sufficient intimation of the "table under the glass," did not sufficiently take into account the resistance of the table, the elasticity of the wood, did not place you sufficiently at the point of shock. The measure of a man's power in a café would have been to prevent the women around him from raising their glasses. Mysteries of gravity. Suppose I hold a plumb line over a painting laid horizontally and open my eyes: if the painting is a "Rembrandt," the plumb will oscillate along the vertical axis, in other cases it will describe a little circle at the center, a "Derain" was supposed to make it move diagonally.[1] Over an ordinary table, at all events, nothing happened. The same experiment would have been just as conclusive in music, in literature, etc. It was, moreover, a time to reconcile the alleged words of God: "Let there be light . . ." and the famous occult dictum: "There is no high. There is no low," that is, to reconcile the most obscure words of all. It was, I don't know why, the time to make a person convinced of these things, enter *into* a canvas, rather than to draw him *out of* the canvas. Not . . . and this is rather contradictory . . . without having painted him as one hangs

1. Nothing of the sort happened, we may be sure.

178

one's overcoat on a hanger. The dream, in spite of Picasso, was to "generate the straight line with cotton." The modern dilemma, paradoxically and admirably expressed: "Beyond all calculations about time, there is the felt hat," said Derain.

Parallel to the feeling that made some of us a prey to such aphorisms, which was, I repeat, based upon the idea that our contact with existing things had been superfluous or excessive, and that contact with other things was indispensable, in the course of that strange enterprise of disenchantment and enchantment to which we are still more or less committed, we verified almost everything, as a man pinches himself in a dream to make sure he is not asleep. The soft hat is not as soft as people say and only *à la rigueur* is it a hat. A hat is not the definite envelope of a head. To be more sinister, I add that a head adheres to the shoulders only because the blade of the guillotine is withheld. The guillotine itself, because I have never seen it, has perhaps never functioned. I know two kinds of painters: those who believe in the skin and those who do not believe in it. I have it from Derain that for him it would have been a lie to paint a woman "without tits and without an ass." Very fortunately Max Ernst's concern at that time and insofar as honesty was involved, was with the solution of an entirely different problem.

Vestibule for vestibule, I shall never forget that at the now remote time of our first meeting, Ernst told me of his certainty at having seen an overcoat or a hat, without the outward participation of anyone whatsoever, leaving one hatrack for another more than a yard away. The incident occurred, I believe, at Cologne, and, under the conditions in which we tried to make it repeat itself, we obtained no result. It is true, however, that on this occasion Max Ernst was less interested in the authenticity of certain phenomena of levitation than in telling me how impossible it was for him to hang anything up in a fixed place, or to believe that a person painted by him, even supposing that he divested himself of this person as of a garment, would stay where he had put him, and not descend from his frame and return to it according to the requirements of the drama that we perform for ourselves.

Lyricism, by which every work that we admire recommends itself, is not by nature indefinable, and if criticism hesitates to push its customary little investigations as far as the lyrical, it is not for fear of profaning what goes straight to our heart: it is from incompetence pure and simple. Seven or eight years ago that pseudo-laboratory, in which certain of the men who have since that time gone most astray, were then involved, indulged in rather unconsidered ramblings on this theme. Through those of their words that have not yet escaped me I disentangle a strikingly concerted endeavor, on the part of several men, to seize the reins of this runaway horse, if only to prevent it from running away again. They questioned Picasso and Chirico as they questioned Rimbaud, there was a mad scramble to seize the head of the horse that was galloping so fast. They also questioned Derain, who boasted of having broken the charger and displayed him, eyes turned heavenward, trampling the earth with hooves still full of sparks. That was lyricism. Something that could be trained and that some people even claimed to have trained. *Recipes*, varying with the selected mode of expression, slipped from drawer to drawer in this hideous kitchen, like birds that have spied the food cupboard. There survive from that period, in the form of practical and irritating recommendations, a thousand and one methods of adapting to the most advanced taste of the day in accordance with the appropriate resources of surprise, of weakness which so often triumphs over strength, of the rape of words so old they can only be rejuvenated, of the prismatic play of light and shadow, of permanent concealment and laughable discovery, of discrediting the modern by the ancient and of discrediting the ancient by forgetting both the modern and the ancient, of an infuriated dialectic that returns the scent of the thorn for the prickle of the rose, of all this there survive a few wild-looking relics, if only that colorprint on the wall of Picasso's studio, from which Seurat seems to have drawn such ironic, such literal inspiration for painting *The Circus* (one cannot help wondering whether his alleged technical achievement in the realm of "composition" is really significant), appeals which take good care not to be cries, and a few tempting locks without keys.

When Max Ernst arrived, these diverse elements were outrageously simplified. He brought with him the unreconstitutable fragments of the labyrinth. It was like creation playing solitaire: all the pieces, broken up in the most fantastic way, no longer finding in each other any particular mutual magnetism, strove to discover new affinities. A diluvial rain, gentle and certain as the twilight, began to fall. To an increasingly parsimonious use of words, in which color was denied and only two tones recognized: hot and cold; in which people no longer thought of agreeing about anything except the meaning of: window, road, sky, con-

nected at most by a sort of screen as at the cinema, — Max Ernst opposed a vocabulary which truly embraced all words, though it reserved the right to dispense with the meaning of several of them and — scandal! — with what lends them a more or less emotional value. The pipe, the newspaper, which is not even tomorrow's, and the guitar are just about washed up. It is known how he proceeded. From Rimbaud's famous love for the decorative panels over doors, for silly refrains, and revolutions of morals, from the systematic taste that Lautréamont is supposed to have had for a sort of spiritual gutter extending from Young to certain medical reports, from Jarry's insulting knowledge of heraldry, and even from the inspiration which Apollinaire sought in catalogues, Max Ernst seems to have inherited the sense of culture as something extraordinary, captivating, paradoxical and priceless. In his collages, the first of his works that are known to us, he no longer, as had been done up until then, tried to use compensating materials (wallpaper [*papier peint*] for painted canvas, scissors stroke for what distinguishes it from the brush stroke, that is, glue spots in the place of painting); instead, he utilized elements endowed in themselves with a relatively independent existence, and so constituted that, for example, photography alone can give us a lamp, a bird or an arm. He did nothing less than regather these disparate objects in an order different from their own, an order from which all in all, they did not seem to suffer, and as far as possible to avoid any preconceived design, and with the same eye with which from your window you watch a man walking on a roof with an open umbrella, with the same state of mind that is needed to think that a windmill can, without the slightest disproportion, serve as a woman's headdress, since this happens in Bosch's *Temptation,* to establish between beings and things considered as given *in favor of the image,* other relations than those which are commonly established, just as in poetry lips can be likened to coral, or reason described as a nude woman casting her looking glass in a well.

There is no doubt that these elements, gathered in a room, in the country, in a factory or in the sea, are not entirely at the mercy of the human act which in representing them confronts them with one another. Those among us who have watched the development of Max Ernst's work, have sometimes seen them take hostile attitudes and become horrified at finding themselves in each other's presence. It was necessary, indispensable, that this should be so. Is it not indeed fitting that the horror which is inspired in us by things here below ("Nature! Nature!" we sob, "the hawk rends the sparrow, the fig eats the donkey and the tapeworm devours man!") is it not fitting that this horror should take hold of us when we consider certain episodes in the dream of Max Ernst, which is a dream of *mediation?* The hostile disjunction of some of the parts is, here again, apt to decide us to risk all for all. Therein perhaps resides for Max Ernst the possibility of living, of living free, and this perhaps is the root of his profound humanity. I like to assure myself that he suffers from the same things as I do, that the obscure cause to which we devote ourselves is not won for him any more than for me. What moves him moves me, and what penetrates to him is sometimes beyond me. Everything that he has absolved from the absurd oath to seem or not to seem, everything upon

which his hands have opened or closed, is all I wanted to see in this way and equal to anything I have seen. Sometimes, one of these constructions, undesired by life, might founder on the mysterious beach of the soul, but often one of these scenes, one of these creatures the revelation of which we dared not expect even from him, grew, grew in our light, became animated with a life that always remained to be lived over again. And these were: *Revolution at Night, 2 Children are menaced by a Nightingale, The Great Lover.* People will no doubt find fault with this selection, the least restrictive of all, and maintain that these three paintings are among those of Max Ernst which develop the most naturally and whose component elements present the minimum of heterogeneity. To this I shall reply that it fits into my system with regard to Max Ernst that the willed encounter on each of his canvases of objects previously disqualified and *drawn at random,* does not exclude the possibility of an anterior encounter on the plane of "reality," that it is perhaps this risk above all that I like to run with him, that it is perhaps this feeble probability in him that I find lyrical *par excellence,* as in the case of my own existence, I should be tempted to count on what may destroy it, only in order to risk some day rediscovering it, to any extent whatever.

But the human head that opens, takes flight, and closes on its thoughts like a fan, the head falling on its hair like a lace pillow, the fragile, weightless head which maintains its balance between the true and the false, crenelated with blue like the dolls of New Mexico, the head whose mask will be molded after my death, this head around which Max Ernst revolves is like the river that will never meet a dike.

The rationalism and mysticism that dispute Derain's soft hat are beneath the feet of Max Ernst.[1]

There is no reality in painting. Virtual images, corroborated or not by visual objects, are more or less effaced beneath our gaze. We can consider painting only as we consider such hypnagogic visions as: *"I compared the aspect of the eyes in that terrible head to that of the bits of red tinfoil that are wrapped around the ends of chocolate cigars, and the brown color of that head itself reminded me of those same cigars"* (Guyon). And yet this sort of hallucination is less edifying than those in which Max Ernst, not without irony, has recently indulged. As for visions, it is certain that we have none. Whether or not we express, in the absence of what is, in the presence of what is not, our desire to dispense both with what we are deprived of and what we are given, whether this sterile, derisive classification is accomplished with or without us, we can only praise Max Ernst for having, on the basis of the illusions to which for example our mediocre steregnostic sense exposes us, built the second part of his work which extends from his *Natural History* to *Vision induced by a piece of string that I found on my table.* It would have been useless to rebel against the exterior distribution of objects, if it was not one day to interrogate something other than the shadow of these objects, and if painting did not in part consist in imprinting upon canvas the effigy of those objects which on a plane canvas surface participate, as I have no doubt, in the tactile

1.

1

Dans un coin l'inceste agile
Tourne autour de la virginité d'un petite robe.
Dans un coin le ciel délivré
Aux pointes des anges laisse des boules blanches.

Dans un coin plus clair de tous les yeux
On attend les poissons d'angoisse.
Dans un coin la voiture de verdure de l'été
Immobile, glorieuse et pour toujours.

A la lueur de la jeunesse
Des lampes allumées très tard
La première montre ses seins que tuent des insectes
rouges.

II

Dévoré par les plumes et soumis à la mer
Il a laissé passer son ombre dans le vol
Des oiseaux de la liberté.
Il a laissé
La rampe à ceux qui tombent sous la pluie.
Il a laissé leur toit a tous ceux qui se vérifient.

Son corps était en ordre,
Le corps des autres est venu disperser
Cette ordonnance qu'il tenait
De la première empreinte de son sang sur terre.

Ses yeux sont dans un mur
Et son visage est leur lourde parure.
Un mensonge de plus du jour,
Une nuit de plus, il n'y a plus d'aveugles.

I

In a corner agile incest
Revolves around the virginity of a little dress.
In a corner the sky surrendered
To angel points deposits white balls.

In a lighter corner of all eyes
We await the fishes of anguish.
In a corner the carriage of summer verdure
Motionless, glorious and forever.

In the light of youth
Lamps lighted very late
The first displays its breasts killed by red insects.

II

Devoured by plumes and submitted to the sea
He let his shadow pass in the flight
Of the birds of liberty.
He left
The ramp to those who fall beneath the rain.
He left their roof to those who verify themselves.

His body was in order,
The body of others came and dispersed
This ordinance that he held
From the first imprint of his blood on earth.

His eyes are in a wall
And his face is their heavy necklace.
One lie more by day,
One night more, there are no more blind.

(Paul Eluard: *Max Ernst.*)

differentiation of flat objects: nervation of the leaf, caning of the chair, caprice of the thread unrolling from a bobbin.

It is thus that after having revolutionized in their relations objects which were at first considered in an elementary way and virtually "rendered" according to their dictionary meaning, with the good faith of a Rousseau enlarging a postal card without other ambition than to make a child designating this spot say the word: lion or the word: cloud; after having abstracted them from what in many cases is mere convention, like the cock over the belfry, or ephemeral like the wax statutes that have not yet left the workshop of the manufacturer to take their place, some in the windows of department stores, others at the Musée Grevin; after having thus enabled us to behold the formation of new beings, no more hybrid or monstrous than the aloes, the sphinx, the apteryx, or than a modern barrel-hooping machine, Max Ernst has now begun to interrogate the substance of objects, to give it full license to determine afresh their shadow, their attitude and their form. Under his brush are born heliotrope women, superior animals attached to the ground by roots, immense forests towards which a savage desire impels us, young people with no other thought than to trample their mothers.

The paintings in this new manner will probably be subjected to the same risks and will incur the same marvelous adventures as the preceding ones. A kind of natural evidence, totally unpredictable, will choose among them. Here again super-reality (*surréalité*) and not reality will claim its rights. If, one day or another, Max Ernst should happen to remind us more gravely of *this life*, and to move us in proportion to the force of the reminder, we shall at least know by what admirable corridor we are returning thither as though returning to a former life. It will not be too soon.

Let us await impatiently the progress of Max Ernst to another and still another period, as it is oddly said in speaking of painters, let us wait to see realized the synthesis of all the true values which it will have been given him to recognize in his domain and to enable us to recognize in turn, and let us pass the sponge over the blackboard of what I have just said, before tracing one of those magnificent rose windows, similar to those in which Raymond Lulle delighted and to which these immortal propositions carried him:

The phantom is an abstract likeness of things created by the imagination.

Digestion is the form in which the digester digests the digestible.

Meaning is the revelation of secrets expressed by the sign.

Beauty is a certain specious form, perceived by sight, hearing, imagination, conception or delectation.

Novelty is a form, by virtue of which the subject is habituated to new habits.

Shadow is the habit of privation of light.

Creation in Eternity is the idea: and in time is the creature.

Comprehension is resemblance to Infinity and apprehension of finity.

The Fourth Visible Poem
by Paul Eluard

(*"The 8 Visible Poems*[1] *composed by Max Ernst in 1931 have been, as faithfully as possible, illustrated by 8 Visible Poems by Paul Eluard in 1946"* [from the publisher's note to "A l'Interieur de la Vue 8 Poèmes," by Max Ernst and Paul Eluard, Paris, 1947.])

1. I.e., collages.

I

And if we are in midwinter I walk on the bank of a river. And if I see a woman fall and drown, the harshness of the cold does not prevent me from going to her rescue. On the stripped trees each ice-needle illumines a morning light.

And if we are in midsummer I notice through my window a woman undressing in a poor room, badly lighted by a pink lamp which she extinguishes as soon as she is nude.

I have nothing but a variable scale for each night but the sum of my nights is in equilibrium. It gives me the assurance of a moral body.

II

The song rises with the tower and lengthens with the woman who lies down, smiling, infinite and beautiful as the sea. I am happy near her, playing on the sand with the sea-weed of her hands, braving the blue wave of her undone hair and the foam of her belly which seem to tell me: retire.

In this vaporous region, in these spaces made iridescent by fairies you come toward me, wide and generous, pink and red, mauve and violet under the surface of your whiteness.

And the horizon suddenly diminishes and tightens around us.

Late in the night I awaken and I listen to you. You are sleeping and complaining or muttering, depending on your being calm, agitated, forgotten or stormy.

III

My eyes were peopled with men and women, distant, disdainful, as intimidating as possible. By exception this was not a holiday, not even one of those good old faded days where I live back into the charms of the past.

All faces were closed. Under the tight and faultless skin the bitter fruit of the skull ripened its prominent grimace.

I wanted to sing of the shadow, to preside over the disorderly transactions of rottenness, over the great councils of poison, over the last convulsions of the roots, over dying adolescents.

But I struck a pebble and my song finished in stupor.

IV

Now comes the giant who will grow, who will perish. Initials have great patience, they orient forever the words which they command.

On the thick table, caught by its angles, the letters trample.

We leave the foolish races to the devotees of rapid calculation, to the intrepid breathers, to the tickling jockeys. The soft rump of rest fulfills our wishes.

V

A pretty world adorned with white sails and which eternalizes while sleeping.

When one has lived for twenty years and believes himself mortal, what about it? Sleep grants time to the sun.

VI

The earth and the clouds tilled by the bright countrywomen, the deprived jawbones of the reflected worker, the gentle distractions of the poet who with difficulty believes himself in a possible world, the courtesan's taste for the theatre, everything goes from the sonorous to the shrill, from the indubitable to the illusory and from the illusory to the real stripped of its weapons and its shield.

VII

At the place where the warm forehead weighs on the pillow, a cunning sunray made a cinders' kernal dance. The fire in the brushwood lifted its skirt over its black stockings, shooting sparks. A mouth wide open with pain, and mute, blew without emitting air. And the strangled tongue spouted with the effort of the most vague of enslaved headsmen.

Later, much later, some turbulent grains of pollen found themselves again on the banks of dawn and I felt in myself the strength of a man, a beating heart, a primitive desire.

VIII

A thousand chimerical projects, only to bounce sadly on the wings of symmetry, on the reflections and replicas of banal movement, on the nullity of time.

I have lost all: my laugh, my tears and my skin of azure. And this laboring field where the vessels of fire loaded with hailstones ran under the tempest. And these spotted trees, of which one fruit limits the earth, another the sun. And my ears at the departure of chaste silence and the meeting of the first germ. And my variegated eyes, diabolically feminine. And these other stars too, which are worn in summer in the cool caverns. And these droll animals who perfectly respond to my desire to change everything.

I have lost all in this mirror where one bakes the daily bread, where, in the shadow, one reproduces my secrets, to infinity.

Max Ernst
by Georges Ribemont-Dessaignes

If there is any label that it is dangerous to apply today, it is that of surrealism. If the wind of public opinion is allowed to buffet it at will, the term may be nothing but a slap in the face of the lucky beneficiary.

If, in connection with Max Ernst, I take it delicately between my thumb and forefinger, it is because surrealist painting would not exist without him. But it cannot be said that Max Ernst would not exist without surrealism. His finest productive period runs parallel to Dada. For my part, I cannot recall without emotion those admirable little scenes in which mystery, with the most extraordinary unconcern, operates outside the realm of shadows. A mystery born of the undirected confrontation of the simplest and most precise forms. We are far removed from the spectral twilight dear to other painters. We find ourselves in a universe which grows out of ours from the point of view of space, but the *deus ex machina* is not the same. He has been switched in infancy, and his amiable successor handles his tools in his own way.

The strangest part of it is that this manner often borrows the aspect of a tragic art which, though hardly in the manner of Corneille, permeates your spirit and flesh without deception.

Before this vision we stand as before a miracle of nature: nothing in nature was devised in the intention of appealing to our emotions. It is the same with Max Ernst's act of creation. Lovers of allegory *must* be disappointed. If they are not, it is because there are titles, and when there is a title and a picture, it is always possible to make up a little story. Putting aside the interpretations cherished by these Messieurs, the association that strikes us most readily verges on poetry. Max Ernst is a poet. But his constructions are of a plastic order (this to reassure the art-lover!) in the sense that he evolves forms, not in relation to their meaning and name, but through a mysterious plastic affinity that he finds in them, the metaphysical charm of which we experience later.

Painters, when they want to be, are the surest propagandists of metaphysics. If I were a usurper among the divinities of any order whatsoever, I should employ the services of a painter. And beyond a doubt, my first choice would be Max Ernst.

Max Ernst and his Reversible Images
by Tristan Tzara

On the occasion of his recent exhibition at the Galerie des Cahiers d'Art (1934).

Is it the cloud of birds flying earthward or the specter of a summer dripping along oars of tears? A dog bays in the night. A child forgotten on the deserted beach, far from the night and the cold pebbles of its breasts. A white spot in the night stretches out to the sea, cravatted in the mourning of the low tides. A dog bays like a tree undressing in fragments of fugitive questions. In the imprescribable desolation of the fruit-bearing assizes, the child finds the compact heat in which his sharp jaws blossom. A constant vibration of clockwork inhabits the game bag of the hurried traveler. But the baying of the dog. There was a lighted window in the night behind which a youth called the double of his anguish which, like an incestuous image cowering in wait to reveal its nudity, dispersed the distant echo of its animality through the sandy expanse. A step, powerful and regular, padlocked the round. The flowers wore delicate dancing slippers and by their mincing trot one measured the importance of the men who

had upside down trees for beards, while tiny little fans wounded the sumptuous air with their careless flight; but the baying of the dog; we had not reckoned with the weather that might prevail on the frontiers of facile purity. The thread of memories immediately present beneath the layer of irises, detestable behind the fence, still flashed its mother-of-pearl teeth and fancied its tawdry parturitions in the sudden light of a semblance of truth.

Thus in the viviparous soul there develops the obsession of an abominable childhood memory, predisposing man's movements and ferruginous action to a maniacal frenzy. It is from the mediocrity of little flames that the grandeur of a unanimous liberating thrust is deduced. Beginning with the little mechanisms of sensory appearance and the schematized tics of scarcely human movements, — so vastly do they multiply by series of perspectives that they seem to be cut up into segments within a single mass that loses itself in the infinite, — passing the echelons of categories and elements, the road leads infallibly to the universal planes of emotions and eternal discoveries. The essential is not so much to recognize the vast array of forces and tempests in what is infinitely small, but rather to incorporate the latter into the destiny of man, by adjusting it, bag and baggage, to the scale of his understanding.

No one better than Max Ernst has understood how to turn the pockets of things inside out. Beneath the benign aspect of a gentleness which is eminently repellent to those who know the hypocrisy it masks, but which, accumulated and administered in massive doses, achieves its opposite, cruelty, under the deceptive aspect of seductive, anachronistic movement, there lies a latent drama: it consists in divesting of their affective content all the symbolic phenomena with which present-day society has cushioned things and creatures. But the polemic value of this action ceases to be anything more than an invisible web when it concerns itself with those operations of amalgamation by which the elements of one realm draw their vitality from other realms, those operations of proliferation the meaning of which boils and bubbles until it exceeds the pictorial and turns into thinking reality. I shall not describe here the curve by which one of the most absolute scepticisms, expressed pictorially by Max Ernst, succeeds, within the framework of its proper medium, in negating this initial negation and moving on an unforeseen plane towards a new universality. It might be said that a movement of this order must be coupled with the basic association whereby every specialized branch of art automatically participates in poetic knowledge, not in an imitative Wagnerian or Orphic sense, but in the intrinsically active and passive sense of the deforming whirlpools which create unprecedented modes of knowledge.

The varying degrees of permeability of man's nature would themselves suffice to justify the divergent and discontinuous efforts of a spirit exposed to such versatile book-keeping as the laws of compensation and the faculties of interpenetration inherent in the elements of nature at its various stages of evolution, permitting man to remain *more* or *less* aloof from all the things around him which conspire to discredit his principle of autonomy. Such is this diversity of human efforts that worlds imbricated on other worlds, in the midst of a broad immensity which alone

preserves a character of unity, fully participate in the mental life of the individual, by plunging him into their swarming life whenever he rises to the light of consciousness or *singularizes* himself by attempting to rule over them. Max Ernst sets out explicitly to demonstrate the vanity of such a pretension. By reversing the face of things to the point of demoralizing them in their essence, and by reducing to diagrams — the irony of whose mechanical techniques stigmatizes the dehumanization of phenomena — violent passions in their traditional and social aspects, Max Ernst reminds man of his larval function as a link in the chain of historic determinism and of the impotence that characterizes any desire to escape from this function individually by the sole force of the idea. By *isolating* the human event, he reduces it to a low position in the hierarchy of the ridiculous, while at the same time he raises it so far as to imbue it with the value of a permanent symbol. To give body to the conciliation of these opposites, Max Ernst sacrifices the generally admitted bases of pictorial art and, broadening the scope of the problem, makes use of impersonal materials, taken by surprise, ready-made or anonymous, worn by wind and rain, which fit like gloves every new circumstance to be expressed, and lend themselves to it out of the pure delight of a random object encountered by a man out for a walk. For these images are based on the optical illusion of a popular need which has fashioned them or found them in the guise of witticisms in the retarded attics of subtle memory.

There is a pictorial pact which binds the painter to a cosmogony of the laws of optics. Before one has finished mixing the elements in a hat and drawing them out blindfolded, they take their place on the canvas in accordance with a formation of equivalents, balanced volumes, and stable color relations, under the hand that sees and the eye that acts. Each element lands on its feet, each one takes its place in its proper constellation, like the planes of crystals in the process adequate to their formation. Such is the rigidity of this visual contract that conventional pictorial material does not resist the exhaustion of objective reality or that reality which can be made objective, and the painter seeks a means of expressing himself in new subject matter, often of the most unexpected character. But the circuit closes when the pictorial matter regains its mode of expression under the new conditions, *despite* the surrounding reality which is now dismembered, dissociated and stripped of its prerogatives which only man's habitual love of comfort causes to pass as the pivot of unshakable solidity.

When the appearance of things and creatures pales, when it undermines vision by the diminution of meaning to which it is submitted in its acute angles or, on the contrary, cushioned by the dust it raises in its flight towards extension, it breaks down into segments of references and, en route, imposes itself on the toothed eye as an incongruous and apparently absurd definition of the natural and manufactured solid, when the propagation of its rash catabolism acts, and quite rapidly, oh cry from afar, on the springs of everything it touches in any way, and most especially takes the form of a perturbation of the shapes inscribed by the passage of famished objects through space governed by a great clatter of light and soapy kettle-drums, beginning with man and ending in rain, frost and oblivion, when a slow mutilation of appearance, symptomatic and

functional, prefigures in its broad outlines putrefaction from the bottom up which, at the same time, is revealed as a sublimation from the top down, and the anomaly of so-called substantial rigidity leaves the spectator the vilest or most exalted possibilities of rectifying the dimensions of the thing that confronts him as an object of sensation — this premium for the return of the assured order of the spiral, the engulfment and expulsion of which are human attainments but which, by its tension, engages the state of the universe in its strict conformation, — when the appearance of things and creatures is thus subjected to a law of sumptuous, systematic and indeterminate deformation, to a prolongation of its necessity in the domain of adjacent realms, the time is ripe, not only to proceed to the implication of these actions for the very nature of man, for his brute substance or his manner of seeing, but also to verify that constant flight of reality, which, alone, by the powers of transmission of one sense on another, seems to assume a power of coordination over the matter around it, a certain rounded quality in an imperious space, which in actual fact it does not possess in itself, since, as fluctuating as our modes of knowledge, it is constantly exchanging its form for its content or conversely, and since outside of these modes it is not conceivable, just as our own being can not take its place in the world which surrounds it and which it surrounds except if it sees itself as essentially mingled with the intimate nature of that world.

On this basis, the modern painter has developed the principle according to which the content and the form of a work are identifiable, just as the techniques employed to this end are confounded with its expression. The subject and the object, by mutually negating each other, give rise to a third entity, which is another expression, richer in implications than that which was bound up with the original meaning, of which, however, it has not ceased to be a part. It necessarily follows that this work is sufficient to itself in the sense that it has no need of any figurative justification of the external world, since, being an act of knowledge, like poetry, it reaches a point where it transforms the vision of the world, or modifies it in in-accordance with an angle peculiar to it-self and in the measure of its own powers, which it imposes in a manner that is all the more virulent in that its radiation is not of brief duration, in other words, in that it applies to the essential structure of this world and not, through subterfuges of propaganda or publicity, to its external form. Its efficacy will be all the greater in that its mode of expression will not be aimed at reason. But that will not prevent it from being reasonable in its evolution, and in its capacity as an integrating force, capable of encrusting itself profoundly in the world of the spirit as an active ele-ment, equally constructive and destruc-tive. The channel by which it chooses to enter into the consciousness of man is infinitely varied; it ranges from directly experienced obsession to the simulation of this obsession, passing through the inter-mediate states which are the characteris-tics of *humor*.

Thus, what is *human* in the work of Max Ernst is defined by the variation of the states of stimulation of direct experi-ences and by the discovery of a new de-gree of humor, that synthetic element which results from the comparison of op-posite terms, negated in their function as significant designations, and constituting

a stage more advanced than the meta-phor, in the sense of a concrete adaptation to vital necessities and of a humanization of their means of exchange, which are made available to man both as vehicles and expressions of his desires.

The security which a finished work gives its author is perceptible only outside him, for it has very little consistency if we consider it as the stamping of a coin which has currency only for a very brief time. Its exchange value exists only at the instant when the work is realized and when its object as well as its subject, which constitute the items to be ex-changed, are negated, that is, when they have completed the act of identification in passing to a higher plane than that on which they originated. And thus we shall have circumscribed one of those pro-visional moments which, multiplied and successive in time, determine the tra-jectory proper to all human activity. It is with this provisional and temporary character of a work of art that we must associate the quality of *despair* which permeates it even in its most secret fibres.

Max Ernst, in the glacial silence of a rigorous introspection, whether at the inert point or at the static point of dream-ing or waking, has most vividly illus-trated that poetic activity which is defined, from the viewpoint of knowledge, as an unsystematized delirium of interpretation or as a continuous relation between psychic simulation and mimetism on the one hand, and the obsessional and irra-tional personality the residue of which is to be decanted. This activity, when it is limited to reversible meanings, finds in their very mobility inventive resources sufficient to identify them as powerful means of subversion and sabotage towards the actual world and towards its reality.

The works of Max Ernst represent, in the multiplicity of their components, a coherent, closed system of thought, in which the undirected means of expression used, mutually determine each other. They are not directed towards any wretched aesthetic pleasures, but constitute an answer to precise desires and real needs. They result from a profound penetration of the signs applying to the laws of nature, and those relating to the dubious conditions of human dignity. In the magic atmosphere that they brew around us, dogs no longer fill the piercing night with their instructive howls. Children find themselves at liberty in bouquets of anchors. Nights are sewed to lightless windows and on the sea as on the land a youthful world burns with all the pride ever experienced and with every incandescent, satisfied nostalgia.

I see Max Ernst, seated like a tailor, patiently hemming with the margins of wells the daylight which has just been cast anew over the shoulder of the earth like tresses wound from memories of the marvelous, defunct beauties of women in panoplies, while on a riotous morrow eyelashes beat frantically through an ineffable freshness of hummingbirds, deep at the bottom of the sea, restored to public life thanks to the scarring over of its wounds.

Max Ernst *by Julien Levy*

Fancies of real validity in childhood have been discarded for the experiences of adult life, but in a hidden corner of Ernst's mind they have been preserved and have reached an unearthly maturity of their own. It is as if Alice were to grow up in Wonderland while you yourself became a stockbroker, and you were to meet her one day, to re-discover her enchantment, now filled with love and terror. Max Ernst became her guardian when you had forgotten her. His hair has always been prematurely an exceptional blue-grey and his eyes have always been young. He burns like the filament of an old fashioned incandescent light. He plays like a child at being grown up, at having a complicated intellect, at being diabolic. He is the oldest innocent. He is rapid and instinctive as a bird and pretends to hate birds. In his paintings he does not (as Paul Klee) imitate the motifs of children. But he develops the child's approach, combined with an adult perfection. From *cut-outs* he has perfected collage. In daubing and rubbing and *finger painting* we find the basis of that technique which he calls *"frottage."* Ernst's paintings are a mass of vibrating colors, having slight likeness to any object, but nevertheless seeming to offer a sort of *essence* of the spirit of the essence of an object. A bird — vari-coloured plumage, flight, brightness, fluttering, excited blood that races so many times faster than the pulse of man. Ernst's fictive objects emerge from his canvas alive, to haunt one and to continue living as long as man has nostalgia for the first appearance of things. Alice and the Red Queen, the Sleeping Princess, Thumbelina, Undine, Pinocchio, all are eternal. So are Loplop, King of the Birds, or *Ma Soeur Germinal, La Femme 100 Têtes*. So is his whole fabulous world. Beneath a sun which is not our sun, but which is essentially color and light, lie forests such as we have never seen, a wood made of many sticks, or a tree made of forests. Bright streaks of color flash across the skies like sparks of fireworks; strange creatures, resembling nothing so much as animate tree bark, live with *La Jeune Fille Qui Voulut Entrer au Carmel.* Ernst paints this world with such evocative detail that we firmly believe in its existence.

Beyond Painting *by Paul Eluard*

Towards 1919, when imagination sought to dominate, to subdue the dreary monsters fortified by the war, Max Ernst resolved to bury the old Reason, the cause of so much disorder, so much disaster — not under its own rubbish but under the free representation of a freed world.

It is not far — through the bird — from the cloud to the man; it is not far — through the images — from the man to his visions, from the nature of real things to the nature of imagined things. Their value is equal. Matter, movement, need, desire are inseparable. Think yourself a flower, a fruit or the heart of a tree, since they wear your colors, since they are necessary signs of your presence, since your privilege is in believing that everything is transmutable into something else.

The true materialistic interpretation of the world cannot exclude the one who reports it. Death itself concerns him, the living man, the living world. I do not know if ever a poet was more penetrated by those fundamental truths than Max Ernst. And this is a first reason to consider, to admire this painter as a great poet. Throughout his entire work one finds the will to confound colors, forms, events, sensations, the futile and the mighty, the fugitive and the permanent,

the ancient and the new, contemplation and action, men and objects, time and duration, the element and the whole, nights, dreams and light.

Max Ernst mingled and identified himself with what he shows us. In projecting his vision beyond this crass, insensible reality which we are expected to accept with resignation, he conducts us into a liberated world where we consent to everything, where nothing is incomprehensible.

Max Ernst *by Nicolas Calas*

Looking for love and finding masks.
*Finding accursed masks and having to
    break them.*
Nietzsche: *Dionysian Dithyrambs.*

The psychological question corresponding to the self-portrait is 'Who am I?' When we see a figure covered by a mask we instinctively ask 'Who is it?' In the age of individualism the mask does not symbolize an archetype, as was the case in the dances of the primitives or in the Greek or Japanese theatre, but it hides an individual. The two forms given by Max Ernst to the Sphinx are highly individualized in contrast to the anonymous characters who act in Chirico's pictures. Everything about the Grandee and the Dandy, as these two forms might be called, indicates individuals gifted with highly developed personalities.

In the portrait of the Dandy, called 'Gardenia,' it is as if a window had been opened and we were allowed to look in unnoticed. We are struck by the cubist background turned into a surface three quarters abstract and one quarter baroque. Against it is projected the profile

191

of an effeminate being bearing a distant resemblance to those pictures of personified flowers once so fashionable. But while those anthropomorphic flowers remained purely formal Ernst's creature is intensely alive. At nearer view this monstrous dandy resembles a bird and an insect. Obviously Ernst enjoyed stressing the confusion suggested by different forms, thus giving to ambivalence an intrinsic 'naturalistic' meaning.

The most amazing feature about the new Ernst monster is its eye. Its spiral shape, so suggestive of the Duchamp 'eye,' could be anything from a satire of the dandy's eye-glass to a nail screwed into the head. The identification of an eye with a nail is horrifying and, on the level of pictorial arts, equal to castration. Fortunately the threatening situation has been partly overcome by the monochrome and nocturnal color of the picture, suggestive of a dream. The night-blue of universality is a balm to our over-exposed anxiety. Although this being is thrust upon us rather than placed in its own three-dimensional space, we can avoid its appalling proximity by waking up. Because the creature is close to us and ever drawing nearer, it produces an icon effect. This dandy could be worshipped, but by whom? This sphinx would cease to be itself if it thus betrayed its identity, revealing its most closely guarded secret. If we looked at the picture long enough the eye would start to turn, although this little experiment made popular by Gestalt psychology does not lead us very far. It may be satisfying to know that the gardenia is combined with the effeminate hand, but the pleasant or unpleasant feelings of movements only add to the hallucinatory effect. If monsters exist it is for them to convince us of the reality of their presence. We are reminded of Kafka's 'Metamorphosis': monsters have reappeared in art (not to be confused with disfigurations) and are terribly personal, as contrasted to the archetype character of mythological monsters. There is nothing taboo about Ernst's creatures and their sex-appeal gives them a romantic *beauté du diable* effect. It is because 'Gardenia' is the personification of the evil of nature (Sade versus Rousseau) that this picture is twentieth century in spirit.

The actuality of Ernst's preoccupation is better understood if we realize the lack of all archaism in the representation of the monstrous, which is naturally a tribute to his inexhaustible imagination. What could be more actual, from an aesthetic point of view, than the background, with its oscillation from the desert of abstraction to the dampness of the saturated sylvan life? Modern, too, in the Baudelairean sense, is the Dandy's viciousness. How deep must be the plunge of those who have been overcome by vertigo and carried into the labyrinthine profundity of that enchanting eye! Without paying an exorbitant price for our temerity can we ever hope to discover the secret of that mind? A curtain may fall over the window, or we can turn away, but the spell has been cast and those among the chosen will carry away the image that so unexpectedly visited them.

If after the 'Gardenia' we look at the Grandee 'Euclid' — the mystery deepens. Here, too, the revolt against futile abstractions is apparent. Euclid's baroque costume, so reminiscent of portraits by Holbein — unless it is a reactivation of the child's vision of its grandmother — is a challenge to Euclidean geometry and the use of it made by cubism and abstract art. As for the fig leaf taken off an ancient statue and turned into a mask, it adds a satirical and 'venetian' note to the violent anti-classical spirit of the picture. Caught between the sea of unidentified dreams and a fragrance of life the Euclidean conception appears singularly limited and antiquated. For the contemporaries of Einstein, art should go beyond purely plastic limitations and the aestheticism of Greek geometricians.

When confronted with masked figures we are not interested to know what they see but what they will say. The emphasis is on the mouth. However, the lips of these two sphinxes are sealed with a sexual secret; they are the victims of an anti-Lisa obsession and cannot smile. What makes their presence so disturbing is a sense of guilt emanating from them. Why would one wish to know what they say if one were not oneself so terribly uneasy? Confessions never saved anybody and analysis only killed creation. These pictures exist through a terrific force of concentration Max Ernst has at last achieved in mastering. We can have great confidence in an artist who rises above the sea level of infantile dreams and emerges with his powerful anthropomorphism as one of the most profound interpreters of the world of our time. What saves his abstract pictures from falling into the aridity of conventional non-figurative art is the realistic outcome of his abstract experiments. He will turn the squares of Mondrian into windows and fill them with images; while Matta's adventures in perspective will be reduced to decorative elements of realistic pictures. Finally a cube or a pyramid is covered by a hat decorated by realistic roses.

If we willed strongly enough, the rose would grow out of water, and in the metronome of our brain — suggested by the pyramidal representation of the head — we would feel the pulsation of life carried by tidal waves. Nevertheless, there is no answer to our anxiety, and in our quest for conscious meanings there is no reason to drown ourselves by plunging too far into the unconscious. There is no answer, and all that is needful is the intense concentration such as art seldom achieves, and then only by appealing to forces that combine in a supreme effort — baroque and abstract, night and day, history and reality, dream and mythical reminiscences — thus giving life that powerful animistic interpretation where plants and human beings, insects, birds and fishes are found in the ever-changing appearances of existence as opposed to the death-like rigidity of pure abstraction.

Hellucinations *by Matta*

The fact that man thinks he grasps phenomena is a hallucination. The notion that "man *is*" is in itself a hallucination; manness is nothing but a sickness of apes. Once hallucinations are sufficiently rooted, they become what we call myths, and cease to have outside limits. I mean that the native African who believes in certain kinds of, let us say, supernatural voices actually hears such voices; his myth, his hallucination is perhaps no more "unreasonable" than the present day one that every house ought to have electric refrigeration so that pop can be served chilled.

History is the story of man's various hallucinations; once we think about some of the influential personages in the story — the devil, venus, christ for example — it is plain that they in part owe their existence as historical personages to having been *pictured* by men with a gift for graphic hallucination. The devil, for instance, is the image of a creature, unhuman, still part animal; the devil could not wholly exist before being pictured; and Max Ernst in this sense has given certain images a historical existence.

The myths Max Ernst has made exist only in notebook form, so to speak; though he has invented many things, he has never bothered to exploit any of them. He has the temperament of a philosopher.

The risk in the power to create hallucinations is that they could be exploited by established authority for its own purposes, the way the Church, for instance, uses images to enslave its members. But the power to create hallucinations should not be checked because it is sometimes criminally abused. However, it is true that in the last century religious hallucinations had to be killed by positivism; history had reached the point where it was necessary to retest all our beliefs. But nowadays science knows very well how to test everything, it is once again permissible to create hallucinations, science can always prevent them from becoming tyrannical — except the scientific hallucination.

At the same time science has castrated emotional experience.

We have been reduced to the fact that white is white, black is black, and that all that we can feel is a punch on the nose. This resolves nothing; the teeth of the dragon remain everywhere. All the same, I am violently against St. George. The power to create hallucinations is the power to exalt existence. It can be argued this constitutes a form of madness, but I think that Max Ernst accepts this as part of the task of the artist. The artist is the man who has survived the labyrinth. It is hard to imagine man ever finding happiness without employing his hallucinatory powers. I believe that this is the essential justification of Max Ernst's direction. *To use hallucinations creatively, not to be enslaved by other men's hallucinations, as usually happens.*

The validity of Max Ernst's procedures is supported by the fact that the mind works the same way in dreams. Certainly the mind works this way in primitive cultures. I am sure that a man could die in fire without *feeling* burnt. From the viewpoint of rational history this is unintelligible; to men in primitive societies it is self-evident. In this sense Max Ernst is a primitive man, even if he doesn't live in a primitive society. But what an affinity he feels, for instance, with the Katchina images from Arizona! He insists throughout his work on the right to create his own hallucinations, and to ridicule other hallucinations. His doves constantly remind us how ridiculous it is to suppose that doves regard the world as a place without conflicts.

Max Ernst has lived two Odysseys, the Odyssey of the erotic and the Iliad of the mind.

Bibliography *by Bernard Karpel*

Bibliography *by Bernard Karpel*

This list has been arranged under the following headings: Writings by Ernst, Editorial work, Graphic and illustrative work, Selected references and an addenda on moving pictures. By the artist's specific direction, a record of manifestoes and broadsides to which his name may be found appended has been omitted since these represent very little or even no contribution on his part.

The abbreviations used are: bibl *refers to the bibliographical item so numbered,* col *colored,* ed *editor,* il *illustration(s),* n.d. *not dated,* no nr *number(s),* nouv. ser. *new series,* p *page(s),* por *portrait(s),* [   ] *signifies data not precisely noted, but supplied by the compiler,* * *indicates item is included, in extract or entirety, in this anthology.*

Therefore, reference number 4 (*bibl* 4) means that an article *titled* Arp, containing one *illustration* will be found in Littérature *volume* 3, *number* 19, *pages* 10 to 12 inclusive of the *issue* dated May 1921.

Writings by Ernst:

1. Adamismus. Die Schammade (Dadameter) [no1:16] Feb 1920.

2. Der alte vivisektor. p[2] *In* Dada au grand air (bibl 110).

3. Antwort der Weltbürger an Kurt Pinthus-Genius. Die Schammade (Dadameter) [no1:13] Feb 1920.

4. Arp. 1il Littérature 3no19:10–12 May 1921.

* 5. Au delà de la peinture. 43il Cahiers d'Art 11no6–7:149–184 1936.

6. La chanson des vieux mutins. Création no2:[9] Nov 1921.
   Poem.

7. [Collage, frottage and other definitions] *In* Dictionnaire abrégé du surréalisme (bibl 112).

* 8. Comment on force l'inspiration (extraits du "Traité de la peinture surréaliste"). Le Surréalisme au Service de la Révolution no6:43–45 May 15 1933.
   For modified translation see bibl 19.

9. Dada est mort, vive dada! Der Querschnitt 1:22 Jan 1921.

10. Danger de pollution. Le Surréalisme au Service de la Révolution no3:22–25 Dec 1931.

11. [Enquête sur l'amour: réponse]. La Révolution Surréaliste no12:72 Dec 15 1929.
    Replies to four questions addressed to several writers and artists, including Ernst.

12. Et suivant votre cas; la série des jeunes femmes. 2il Littérature (nouv. ser.) no7:8–9 Dec 1 1922.
    Text by Paul Eluard and Max Ernst.

13. Etna. Littérature (nouv. ser.) no11–12: 17 Oct 15 1923.
    Poem.

13a. La femme 100 têtes. See bibl 46.

14. First memorable conversation with the chimera. 8il VVV no1:17 June 1942.

15. [Foreword]. *In* Levy, Julien, Gallery. Dorothea Tanning. Apr 1944.
    Introductory note for exhibition catalog.

16. Gertrude. Die Schammade (Dadameter) [no1:24] Feb 1920.

16a. L'homme qui a perdu son squelette. See bibl 42a.

17. The hundred-headless woman. View 1no7–8:7 Oct 12 1941.

18. [Il faut visiter l'exposition surréaliste 7 au 18 juin à la galerie Pierre Colle]. [Paris, 1933].
    Introduction to catalog written by Tristan Tzara and Max Ernst.

* 19. Inspiration to order. *In* Evans, Mfanwy, ed. The painter's object. p74–79 London, Gerald Howe, 1937.
    Translation by M. Evans. Also translated in This Quarter p79–85 Sept 1932, and in Art of this century (bibl 122). These are condensed versions of bibl 8.

20. [Interview] 3il(por) Museum of Modern Art Bulletin 13no4–5:16–18 1946.
    Special number of "artists . . . under interview," edited by James Johnson Sweeney as "Eleven Europeans in America." Bibliography, p37.

21. Lisbeth. Die Schammade (Dadameter) [no1:24] Feb 1920.

22. Lukrative Geschichtsschreibung. Die Schammade (Dadameter) [no1:30] Feb 1920.

22a. Les malheurs des immortels. See bibl 48.

23. Man Ray. *In* Six, Librairie, Paris. Exposition dada Man Ray du 3 au 31 décembre 1921.
    Introductory note for exhibition catalog.

*23a. Max Ernst's favorite poets and painters. See bibl 160.

24. Les mystères de la forêt. il Minotaure no5:6 May 12 1934.

25. [Die pensées sans langage. . . .] Die Schammade (Dadameter) [no1:8] Feb 1920.

26. Préface, ou Loplop présente la mariée du vent. *In* Carrington, Leonora. La maison de la peur. p[1–2] 1938 (bibl 66).

26a. Rêve d'une petite fille qui voulut entrer au Carmel. See bibl 50.

27. s'Fatagalied. p[2] *In* Dada au grand air (bibl 110).
    Poem, signed "Arp und Max Ernst (Fatagaga)."

28. Setzt ihm den zylinder auf. Bulletin D no1:2 1919.
    By H. Hoerle and M. Ernst.

* 29. Some data on the youth of M.E., as told by himself. 4il(por) View 2no1:28–30 Apr 1942.
    Also published in New Road (London) p200–3 1943.

30. [Statement]. *In* Aragon, Louis & Breton, André. A suivre, petite contribution au dossier de certains intellectuels à tendances révolutionnaires. p(xv) [Paris, 1929].
    Insert in Le Surréalisme en 1929 special number of Variétés June 1929.

31. [Testimonianze]. p5–6 *In* Guggenheim, Peggy & Alfieri, Bruno. La collezione Peggy Guggenheim. Venezia [Instituto tipografico editoriale] 1948.

32. Über Cézanne. Bulletin D no1:7 1919.

33. Die ungeschlagene fustanella. p[2] *In* Dada au grand air (bibl 110).

34. Visions de demi-sommeil. La Révolution Surréaliste no9–10:7 Oct 1 1927.

35. Vom werden der farbe. Der Sturm 8nr5: 66–68 Aug 1917.

36. Was ist surrealismus? *In* Zürich. Kunsthaus. Ausstellung 11. oktober–4. november. p3–7 1934.
    Introduction to catalog listing 100 works by Arp, Ernst, Giacometti, Gonzalez, Miro.

37. Was die zeitungen mir vorwerfen, ist unwahr. *In* Dada ausstellung. p[4] 1920 (bibl 111).

38. Die wasserprobe. *In* Dada au grand air. p[2] (bibl 110).
    Poem.

39. Worringer, profetor Dadaistikus. Die Schammade (Dadameter) [no1:7] Feb 1920.

See also literary material listed under *Graphic & Illustrative Work.*

Editorial Work:

40. Bulletin D. Edited by Johannes Theodor Baargeld and Max Ernst. Cologne, 1919.
    "Für den inhalt verantwortlich Max Ernst, Köln." Cover, illustrations and reproductions by Ernst. Catalog of exhibition lists items 10–17 by Ernst. Contributions by Ernst (bibl 28,32).

41. Die Schammade. Edited by Johannes Theodor Baargeld and Max Ernst. Cologne, Feb 1920.
    Lettered on cover: Dadameter. Title

page and illustrations by Ernst. Contributions by Ernst (bibl 1,3,16,21,22,25, 39).

42. VVV. Editor: David Hare; editorial advisers: André Breton, Marcel Duchamp, Max Ernst. New York, no1, June 1942–no4, Feb 1944.
Cover for no 1; illustrations in no 1, 4; text (bibl 45,63).

42a. L'Homme qui a perdu son squelette. Roman par Arp, Carrington, Duchamp, Eluard, Hugnet, Prassinos et Ernst. 1939.
Communal literary work, with unidentified individual contributions. Partly published in Plastique no5 1939.

Graphic and Illustrative Work:

43. Brunidor portfolio no1. Introductory essay by Nicolas Calas. New York, Brunidor editions, 1947.
One etching by Ernst, in edition of 75 copies of 7 original prints in folio.

44. Fiat modes: 8 original lithographien. Köln-Rhein, Schlömilchverlag, 1929.
Issued loose in folio.

45. First memorable conversation with the chimera. VVV no1:17 June 1942.
Facsimile of manuscript, with illustrations.

46. La femme 100 têtes. Avis au lecteur par André Breton. Paris, Editions du Carrefour, 1929.
149 collages with captions, issued in edition of 1003 copies. Preface, [6]p. Illustrations printed also in Variétés 2no8: 565–69 Dec 15 1929. See also bibl 17.

47. Histoire naturelle. Paris [Éditions Jeanne Bucher] 1926.
Frottages, issued loose in folio, in edition of 306 numbered and signed copies. Introduction by Hans Arp. Originally advertised as "34 dessins reproduits en phototypie."

48. Les malheurs des immortels, révélés par Paul Eluard et Max Ernst. 43p incl 21il Paris, Librairie Six, 1922.
20 drawings with accompanying text. Frontispiece additional. Translation, bibl 49.

49. Misfortunes of the immortals. 52p il New York, Black Sun press, 1943.
English translation by Hugh Chisholm "supplemented by three drawings twenty

years after." Edition of 600, including 100 signed copies, designed by Caresse Crosby.

50. Rêve d'une petite fille qui voulut entrer au Carmel. Paris, Éditions du Carrefour, 1930.
80 collages, with introduction and captions, in edition of 1060 copies.

51. Une semaine de bonté, ou Les sept éléments capitaux. 5 parts Paris, Éditions Jeanne Bucher, 1934.
"Ce roman . . . est une suite de 188 gravures reproduites en phototypie." Collages issued in five parts: 1, Le Lion de Belfort. — 2, L'Eau. — 3, La Cour du Dragon. — 4, Oedipe. — 5, Le Rire du Coq, L'Ile de Pâques, L'Intérieur de la Vue, La Clé des Chants. Edition of 828 copies. Copies on Arches contain an original etching.

52. Littérature. (nouv.ser.)no11–12 Oct 15 1923.
Poetry number, with 44 small drawings by Ernst.

53. Mizué. Album surréaliste. Numéro spécial, 1937.
Cover by Ernst. Catalog edited by Shizo Takiguchi and Tiroux Yamanaka for exhibition at Tokio.

54. La Révolution Surréaliste. no1 Dec 1 1924, no2 Jan 15 1925.
Contains articles illustrated by Ernst drawings.

55. Die Schammade. Feb 1920 (bibl 41).
Title page by Ernst.

56. View. ser2 no1 Apr 1942.
Cover by Ernst.

57. VVV. no1 1942.
Cover by Ernst.

58. VVV [Portfolio of eleven original works] New York, Bernard J. Reis, 1942.
Limited edition of 50 copies, including one frottage by Ernst.

59. ARP, HANS. Gedichte: Weisst du schwarzt du. Fünf klebebilder von Max Ernst. Zurich, Pra Verlag, 1930.
Collages completed 1929. Edition of 250 copies.

60. BARON, JACQUES. Paroles. Marseille, Éditions Les Cahiers du Sud, 1932.
Frontispiece by Ernst.

61. BRETON, ANDRÉ. Le château étoilé. Dessins de Max Ernst. 7il Minotaure no8: 25–39 1936.

Minotaure also issued in *1937* a special edition of *50 copies with 8 plates, including an original frottage signed by the artist.*

62. BRETON, ANDRÉ. Manifeste du surréalisme. Poisson soluble. Nouvelle édition. Paris, Éditions Kra, 1929.
Frontispiece by Ernst.

63. BRETON, ANDRÉ. Situation du surréalisme entre les deux guerres, illustré par Max Ernst. 6il VVV no2–3:44–53 Mar 1943.

64. BRZEKOWSKI, JAN. Zacisniete dookota ust. 4il [1934–5?].
Frontispiece and illustrations by Ernst.

65. CARRINGTON, LEONORA. La dame ovale. 7il Paris, G L M, 1939.
Collages by Ernst.

66. CARRINGTON, LEONORA. La maison de la peur. Préface et illustrations de Max Ernst. 3il Paris, H. Parisot, 1938 (Collection "Un Divertissement." 4)
"Préface, ou Loplop présente la mariée du vent," p1–2.

67. CARROLL, LEWIS. Hunting of the Snark. Edited by Henri Parizot. (In process, 1946–   ).

68. CREVEL, RENÉ. Mr. Knife, Miss Fork. Translated by Kay Boyle, illustrated by Max Ernst. Paris, Black Sun press, 1931.
"A fragment of the novel Babylone . . . illustrated with nineteen original photograms." Edition of 255 copies, including 5 special copies containing 4 of the original drawings.

69. ELUARD, PAUL. Au défaut du silence. [Privately printed, 1926].
20 drawings. Edition of 51 numbered copies. "The anonymous illustration has never been identified" (Max Ernst). Ascribed to Ernst by Albert Skira.

70. ELUARD, PAUL. A l'intérieur de la vue, 8 poèmes visibles. 122p incl 39il (some col.) Paris, Pierre Seghers, 1948.
"Les 8 poèmes visibles de Max Ernst composés en 1931 ont été illustrés par 8 poèmes visibles de Paul Eluard en 1946." Drawings and collages reproduced by lithography and hand-colored.

71. ELUARD, PAUL. Les dessous d'une vie, ou La pyramide humaine. Edition ornée d'un portrait par Max Ernst. Marseille, Les Cahiers du Sud, 1926. (Collection "Poètes," no3).

72. ELUARD, PAUL. Mourir de ne pas mourir. Avec un portrait de l'auteur par Max Ernst. Paris, Nouvelle Revue Française, 1924.

73. ELUARD, PAUL. Une personnalité toujours nouvelle . . . 1oil Documents 34 (nouv. ser.) no1:11–15 June 1934.
Illustrations by Ernst in special number Intervention Surréaliste.

74. ELUARD, PAUL. Répétitions. Dessins de Max Ernst. 11il Paris, Au Sans Pareil, 1922.
Edition of 350 copies. Cover, and colored frontispiece also by Ernst. Translation of poem "Max Ernst" (p7) in Contemporary Poetry and Prose no2: 21 June 1936. See also bibl 117.

75. ELUARD, PAUL. Thorns of thunder. Selected poems . . . edited by George Reavey. London, Europa press and Stanley Nott ltd., 1936.
Jacket design by Ernst. Original collage for jacket reproduced in London Bulletin no7:29 Dec 1938–Jan 1939.

76. ELUARD, PAUL. Chanson complète. 4il Paris, Éditions Gallimard, 1939.
20 copies issued with 4 lithographs by Ernst.

77. EXPOSITION SURRÉALISTE. [Paris, Galerie Pierre Colle, 1933].
Design on rear cover formed by fingers of Tzara and Ernst. See bibl 18.

78. FRENCH WAR RELIEF. Calendar. New York, 1942.
Includes one drawing by Ernst.

79. GASCOYNE, DAVID. A short survey of surrealism. London, Cobden-Sanderson, 1935.
Colored jacket by Ernst.

80. GUGGENHEIM, PEGGY. Art of this century. New York, 1942.
Cover by Ernst. See bibl 122.

81. KAFKA, FRANZ. Un divertissement. Traduit par Henri Parisot. Paris, G L M, 1938.
Frontispiece by Ernst.

82. KAFKA, FRANZ. La tour de Babel. Traduit par Henri Parisot. Paris, G L M, 1937.
Drawing by Ernst.

83. KAFKA, FRANZ. *Metamorphose.* (In process) 1946–   .

84. LAUTRÉAMONT, COMTE DE (ISIDORE DUCASSE). Oeuvres complètes. Paris, G L M, 1938.

Illustrations by Ernst, Masson, Miro and others.

85. LÉLY, GILBERT. Je ne veux pas qu'on tue cette femme. Paris, Éditions Surréalistes, 1936.
Frontispiece by Ernst.

86. PÉRET, BENJAMIN. Au 125 du boulevard Saint-Germain, conte. Avec une pointe-sèche de Max Ernst et trois dessins de l'auteur. Paris, Les Presses du Montparnasse, 1923. (Collection "Littérature").
Edition of 181 copies.

87. PÉRET, BENJAMIN. Je ne mange pas de ce pain-la! Paris, Éditions Surréalistes, 1937.
Drypoint by Ernst.

88. PÉRET, BENJAMIN. Je sublime. Paris, Éditions Surréalistes, 1936.
"Avec 4 frottages originaux." Copy 1, on Japan, contained the mss. and 4 original frottages; 15 copies issued with "original" frottages; regular edition of 225 copies. Also advertised as an edition of 345, of which 45 were to be issued with 4 original frottages in colors.

89. PÉRET, BENJAMIN. La mare aux mitrailleuses, suivi de Le passager du transatlantique. Couverture et 10 illustrations par Max Ernst. Préface par André Breton. Paris, Librairie Gallimard [projected].
"Announced for publication, but never issued" (Ernst).

90. TZARA, TRISTAN. Où boivent les loups. Paris, Gallimard, 1936.
Etching by Ernst.

91. TZARA, TRISTAN. Le coeur à gaz. Paris, G L M, 1946.
25 copies with drypoint in color by Ernst. Regular edition of 380 copies.

92. VIOLETTE NOZIÈRES. Bruxelles, Éditions Nicolas Flamel, 1933.
One illustration by Ernst. Edition of 220 copies, of which 10 were issued with a suite, numbered and signed by the participant artists.

Selected References:

92a. ARAGON, LOUIS. La peinture au défi. Exposition de collages . . . mars 1930. 1il p22–24+ Paris, Galerie Goemans, 1930.
Partly published in bibl 136.

* 93. ARP, JEAN. Introduction *In* Ernst, Max.

Histoire naturelle. Paris, Éditions Jeanne Bucher, 1926.

94. BARON, JACQUES. Max Ernst, ou le monde à l'envers. 1il Le Centaure no8: 152–5 May 1 1927.

95. BERNHEIM, GEORGES, GALERIE, PARIS. Max Ernst; ses oiseaux, ses fleurs nouvelles, ses forêts volantes, ses malédictions, son satanas. 6il [10]p 1928.
Catalog of exhibition held Dec 1–15, listing 50 works, with "Préface" by René Crevel, [5]p.

96. BLOCK, MAXINE. Max Ernst. 1il(por) Current Biography 3:14–16 Dec 1942.
Includes brief extracts from biographical statements by the artist, and bibliography.

97. BOSSCHÈRE, JEAN DE. Max Ernst. 5il Cahiers d'Art 3no2:69–73 1928.
Review of exhibit at Van Leer gallery, with prefatory note by [Christian Zervos]. Partly published in bibl 97.

98. BRETON, ANDRÉ. Avis au lecteur pour "La femme 100 têtes" de Max Ernst. *In his* Point du jour. p76–85 Paris, N R F, Gallimard, 1934.
Originally published in bibl 46, later in bibl 136.

* 99. BRETON, ANDRÉ. Les pas perdus. p101–3, 147,156–8,196 Paris, N R F, Gallimard, 1924 (Les documents bleus).
"Max Ernst," p101–3, also in bibl 136.

*100. BRETON, ANDRÉ. Le surréalisme et la peinture. p47–56 10il Paris, N R F, Gallimard, 1928.
Originally printed in La Révolution Surréaliste 3no9–10:38–41 Oct 1 1927. Also published in bibl 101,136.

*101. BRETON, ANDRÉ. Vie légendaire de Max Ernst, précédée d'une brève discussion sur le besoin d'un nouveau mythe. p159–68 *In his* Le surréalisme et la peinture. 1il(col) New York, Brentano's 1945.
Text dated 1942. English translation by Lionel Abel in View 2no1:5–7 Apr 1942.

102. BRETON, ANDRÉ. Max Ernst. See bibl 150.

103. BURCHARD, OTTO, KUNSTHANDLUNG, BERLIN. Erste internationale dada-messe. [4]p 1920.
Extensive exhibition held in June. No. 76,82,83,89,105,115,147 by Ernst.

104. BUTOR, MICHEL. Hommage partiel à

Max Ernst. 4il Vrille no1:[84–88] July 25 1945.
Poem.

105. CALAS, NICOLAS. And her body became enormous luminous and splendid. View 2no1:20–21 Apr 1942.

*106. CALAS, NICOLAS. Magic icons. 2il Horizon 14no83:304–315 Nov 1946.

107. CARRINGTON, LEONORA. The bird superior, Max Ernst. View 2no1:13 Apr 1942.
Also published in New Road p194 1943.

107a. COHEN, WALTER. Max Ernst. See bibl 119.

108. COURTHION, PIERRE. De Böcklin à Max Ernst. 2il Le Centaure 3no2:26,28 Nov 1 1928.

108a. CREVEL, RENÉ. Préface [on Max Ernst] See bibl 95.
First published in bibl 109. Subsequently published in bibl 119.

109. CREVEL, RENÉ. Max Ernst. 7il(por) Der Querschnitt 8no10:711–12 Oct 1928.
Also published in bibl 136.

110. DADA AU GRAND AIR. [4]p 1il [Paris, Au Sans Pareil, 1921].
Leaflet with inverted title which reads: Der Sängerkrieg in Tirol. Tarrenz B. Imst 16 September 1886–21. Includes 4 contributions by Ernst (bibl 2,27,33, 38).

111. DADA AUSSTELLUNG, DADA-VORFRÜHLING. Gemälde, skulpturen, zeichnungen, fluidoskeptrik, vulgärdilettantismus. [4]p [Cologne, 1920].
Catalog of sensational Cologne exhibit, with works by Arp, Baargeld, Ernst, Picabia, etc. Brief texts by Arp, Baargeld, Ernst (bibl 37).

112. DICTIONNAIRE ABRÉGÉ DU SURRÉALISME. p3,7,9,10,12,13,21,23,26,36,40,41,55, 59, 76. Paris, Galerie Beaux-Arts, 1938.
Definitions by Ernst (collage, frottage, etc.) and illustrations. Includes catalog of international exhibition of surrealism (15 works by Ernst) held Jan–Feb 1938, organized by Breton and Eluard. "Special consultants, Salvador Dali and Max Ernst."

113. DREAMS THAT MONEY CAN BUY. il New York, Art of this century films. inc., 1948.
Catalog for film by Hans Richter which won prize at Cinematography Biennale Film Festival 1947. Cover design: collage by Max Ernst from "La Semaine de Bonté." "1st dream . . . Desire. Inspired by Max Ernst's collage in his book, "La Semaine de Bonté." . . . Written, produced, directed, and designed by Hans Richter in cooperation with Max Ernst. Dialogue by Max Ernst. The Part of "Le Président" is played by Ernst. Brief biographical data, p[3]. See also bibl 148.

*114. ELUARD, PAUL. Au delà de la peinture. In his Donner à voir. Paris, Gallimard, 1939.

115. ELUARD, PAUL. L'évidence poétique. Cahiers d'Art 11no6–7:185–8 1936.

116. ELUARD, PAUL. Max Ernst. 5il Cahiers d'Art 10no5–6:102 1935.
Poem.

*117. ELUARD, PAUL. Max Ernst. p9,121 In his Capitale de la douleur. Paris, Librairie Gallimard, 1926.
Poems dated 1922 and 1926, from Répétitions and Nouveaux poèmes. Also published in bibl 136. Translated by George Reavey in Thorns of thunder (bibl 75), in London Bulletin no7:5,7 Dec 1938–Jan 1939, and in bibl 133.

117a. ELUARD, PAUL. Max Ernst. 1 col il p49–53 In his Voir. Genève-Paris, Éditions des Trois Collines [1948].
Includes poems in bibl 117.

*118. ELUARD, PAUL. Le quatrième poème visible. Pour illustrer des collages de Max Ernst intitulés A l'intérieur de la vue. Confluences (nouv. ser.) 5no9:934–7 Feb 1946.
See also bibl 70.

119. FLECHTHEIM, ALFRED, GALERIE, BERLIN. Max Ernst. 12p 8il(por) 1929.
Catalog of exhibition of 55 works held Mar 1929, and in May in Dusseldorf. Essays on Ernst by Dr. Walter Cohen. p2–5, by René Crevel ("aus dem Querschnitt") p7–10, and a statement by Flechtheim.

120. GASCOYNE, DAVID. La semaine de bonté, à Max Ernst. Cahiers d'Art 10no5–6: 102 1935.
English poem translated by Paul Eluard.

121. GASCOYNE, DAVID. A short survey of surrealism. p33–4,52–4,73–6,104–8 et passim London, Cobden-Sanderson, 1935.

122. GUGGENHEIM, PEGGY, ed. Art of this century: objects, drawings, photographs,

paintings, sculpture, collages, 1910 to 1942. p103–5,139–42,149 4il(por) New York, Art of this century, 1942.
Drawing on cover by Ernst. Brief biography and list of works in the collection. Essay by Ernst "Inspiration to order" (bibl 19) and statement, p139–42.

123. GUGGENHEIM, PEGGY. My life with Max Ernst, End of my life with Max Ernst. p265–333 *In her* Out of this century. New York, Dial press, 1946.
"As a source of information, absolutely worthless" (Max Ernst).

124. HILDEBRANDT, HANS. Die Kunst des 19. und 20. Jahrhunderts. p427 1il Wildpark-Potsdam, Akademische Verlagsgesellschaft, Athenaion M.H.B., 1924 (postscript 1931).

125. HUGNET, GEORGES. L'esprit dada dans la peinture. il Cahiers d'Art 7no1–2: 57,65, no6–7:281–5, no8–10:358–64 1932; 9no1–4:109–14 1934.

126. HUGNET, GEORGES. The human form in perspective. 3il XX⁰ Siècle no5–6:19–20 1939.

127. HUGNET, GEORGES. Max Ernst. Cahiers d'Art no5–10:140 1939.
Poem. Pages 141–5 consist of 10 il of sculpture, also published in part in London Bulletin no18–20:23 June 1940 as "House at St. Martin d'Ardeche rebuilt and decorated by Max Ernst."

128. HUYGHE, RENÉ. Histoire de l'art contemporain: la peinture. p343 et passim Paris, Alcan, 1935.
Biography and bibliography previously published in L'Amour de l'Art, Mar 1934. The following corrections have been stated by the artist (Jan 1948): Born at Bruhl near Cologne. — Studied at the University of Bonn. — Influenced by Chirico, not by Picasso or Archipenko. — No exhibition at Galerie Van Leer for 1921. — "Histoire naturelle" is not collage but frottage (drawings).

129. JANIS, SIDNEY. Abstract and surrealist art in America. 2il p124–5 et passim New York, Reynal & Hitchcock, 1944.

130. JANIS, SIDNEY. Journey into a painting by Ernst. 2il View 2no1:10–12 Apr 1942.

131. LECOMTE, MARCEL. Chirico, Max Ernst et Turin. 1il London Bulletin no14:10–12 May 1939.

132. LEVY, JULIEN. The children outside and the children inside. View 2no1:26–7, 31 Apr 1942.

*133. LEVY, JULIEN. Surrealism. 8il p14–15, 99,112,121–5 New York, Black Sun press, 1936.
Includes translation of "Max Ernst," poem by Eluard.

134. LLOYD, PETER. Max Ernst and surrealism. 4il Creative Art 11:214–6 Nov 1932.

135. LONDON GALLERY. Max Ernst catalogue. 7il London Bulletin no7:3–4+ Dec 1938–Jan 1939.
Lists 51 works, followed by poems by Eluard (p5,7) and Péret (p6,8).

*136. MAX ERNST. Oeuvres de 1919 à 1936. 126il(por,1 col) [110]p Paris, Éditions "Cahiers d'Art," 1937.
A major work on the artist, including bibl 5 and 19. Among other contributions, represented partly in extract only, are bibl 92a,97,98,99,100,109,117,143, 145,157,161.

137. MADDOX, CONROY. The object in surrealism. il London Bulletin no18–20:39–45 June 1940.

138. MILLER, HENRY. Another bright messenger. View 2no1:17 Apr 1942.

139. MOESCHLIN, WALTER J. Hommage à Max Ernst. n.d.
"Pour le vernissage de l'exposition de Max Ernst," Galerie d'Art Moderne, Basel. Mimeographed release.

140. MORTENSER, RICHARD S. Max Ernst. 1il Linien 2nr10:8–9 Feb 15 1935.

141. NEW YORK. MUSEUM OF MODERN ART. Fantastic art, dada, surrealism. Edited by Alfred H. Barr, Jr.; essays by Georges Hugnet. 3d ed. 14il (1col) p25–8, 43–4, 250–1, 162–70 et passim New York, Museum of Modern Art, distributed by Simon and Schuster, 1947 (c1936).

142. OZENFANT, AMÉDÉE. [Letter from Amédée Ozenfant on the work of Ernst]. View 2no1:31 Apr 1942.

143. PÉRET, BENJAMIN. Portrait de Max Ernst. Littérature (nouv. ser.) no11–12: 15 Oct 15 1923.
Poem, also published in his Le grand jeu p46 Paris, Gallimard, 1928; London Bulletin no7:6 Dec 1938–Jan 1939 also contains (p8) his poem of the same title dated 1926, and in bibl 136.

144. READ, HERBERT. Art now, an introduc-

tion to the theory of modern painting and sculpture. 4il p138–40 New York, Harcourt, Brace & Co., 1934.

145. READ, HERBERT. Max Ernst. 3il The Listener 9no230:899 June 7 1933.
Also published in bibl 136.

146. RIBEMONT-DESSAIGNES, GEORGES. Dada painting or the oil eye. 4il The Little Review 9no4:11–12 Autumn and Winter 1923–1924.

*147. RIBEMONT-DESSAIGNES, GEORGES. Max Ernst. Cahiers du Sud 16 (numéro spécial) :39–40 Dec 1929.
Special number "La poésie et la critique" with 7il by Ernst throughout issue.

148. RICHTER, HANS. À propos de Max Ernst et de "La semaine de bonté." 2il (col) Style En France no4:96 Nov 15 1946.
See also bibl 113.

149. ROH, FRANZ. Max Ernst und die stückungsgraphik. Das Kunstblatt Nov 1927.

150. SANS PAREIL, PARIS. Exposition dada Max Ernst. 1il 1921.
Catalog of exhibition held May 3–June 3, with introduction by André Breton "Max Ernst," and list of 56 works including "Fatagaga" (Arp and Ernst).

151. SOBY, JAMES THRALL. After Picasso. 3il p80,87–89,95–6,104,112 Hartford, Edwin Valentine Mitchell; New York, Dodd, Mead, 1935.

152. SPARE, AUSTIN & CARTER, FREDERICK. Automatic drawing. Form 1no1:27–30 Apr 1916.

152a. SWEENEY, JAMES JOHNSON. Eleven Europeans in America. See bibl 20.

153. TAKIGUCHI, SHIZO & YAMANAKA, TIROUX, eds. Album surréaliste. 13il Tokio, "Mizué," 1937.
Special number of Mizué with catalog of surrealist exhibition. Text in Japanese, index and bibliography in English.

154. THE TEMPTATION OF ST. ANTHONY. Bel Ami international competition and exhibition of new paintings by eleven American and European artists, 1946–1947. 2il(por,1col) p9 New York, 1946.
"Competition sponsored by Loew-Lewin in connection with the making of the film 'The Private Affairs of Bel Ami,' "

won by Max Ernst who comments briefly.

155. THIS QUARTER. Surrealist number. 1il 5no1 Sept 1932.
Guest editor, André Breton. Includes "Inspiration to order." (bibl 19).

156. TYLER, PARKER. A gift from Max Ernst. 1il View 2no1:16 Apr 1942.

*157. TZARA, TRISTAN. Max Ernst et les images réversibles, à propos de sa récente exposition à la galerie de Cahiers d'Art. 7il Cahiers d'Art 9no5–8:165–71 1934.
Also published in bibl 136.

158. VAN LEER, GALERIE, PARIS. Exposition Max Ernst du 10 mars au 24 mars. 5il [10]p 1926.
Catalog with list of 48 works in several media, and poems by Eluard, Desnos, Péret.

159. VAN LEER, GALERIE, PARIS. Exposition Max Ernst du 15 mars au 5 avril. 4il 1927.
Catalog of 36 works.

159a. VALENTINE GALLERY, NEW YORK [Max Ernst exhibition]. See bibl 160.

*160. VIEW. Max Ernst number 10il 2no1 Apr 1942.
Includes catalog of exhibition held Mar 23–Apr 11 at the Valentine gallery; list of 31 works, illustrated books and bibliography; items noted in bibl 29,101,105, 107,130,132,138,142,156.
The text for "favorite poets and painters" (p14–15) is by Ernst, the typography by Charles H. Ford and the artist.

161. VIOT, JACQUES. Max Ernst. 22il Cahiers d'Art 8no5–6:215–23 1933.
Also published in bibl 136.

162. VITRAC, ROGER. Max Ernst. In Edouard-Joseph, René. Dictionnaire biographique des artistes contemporains 1910–1930. 1:468–70 5il(por) Paris, Art & Édition, 1930.

163. WILENSKI, RALPH H. Modern French painters, p263,276,297 et passim New York, Reynal & Hitchcock [1940].
Includes extract, p276, from bibl 19.

Moving Pictures:

DREAMS THAT MONEY CAN BUY. A film. New York, 1947.
First sequence by Hans Richter and Max Ernst. See bibl 113.

This is the seventh volume in the
series "The Documents of Modern Art."
The type face is Linotype Caslon,
set in 12 point, leaded 2 pts.; the paper
is White Colophon stock. The
composition, letter-press printing
and binding has been done by
E. L. HILDRETH & COMPANY,
Brattleboro, Vermont. The illustrations,
with their captions and folios,
were printed in offset by the
MERIDEN GRAVURE COMPANY,
Meriden, Connecticut.

Cover and typography by PAUL RAND.
Line drawing on cover by MAX ERNST.

Other Publications by Wittenborn, Schultz, Inc.

American Abstract Artists. Essays by J. Albers, A. E. Gallatin, K. Knaths, F. Leger, L. Moholy-Nagy, P. Mondrian, G. L. K. Morris. ill. 1946   2.50

Braque (Georges) by A. E. Gallatin. ill. 1943 out-of-print

Braque (Georges) Still Life, 1913. color silk-screen repr. 1943   6.00

Burliuk (David) by K. S. Dreier. ill. 1944   4.75

Calder (Alexander) The Big "I," etching 1944   20.00

Degas (Edgar) Huit Sonnets. ill. 1946   4.50

The Documents of Modern Art. Director: Robert Motherwell. See cover

Duchamp's Glass by K. S. Dreier and Matta Echaurren. ill. 1944   1.75

Fuller (Sue) Cock, color engraving 1944   20.00

Gallatin (A. E.) Paintings. ill. 1948   4.00

Gallatin (A. E., editor) Of Art, Plato to Picasso. Aphorisms. 1944   1.50

Goll, C. and Y. Love Poems. ill. by Marc Chagall.   3.00 and 25.00

Hayter (Stanley William) Flight, engraving 1944   30.00

Kjersmeier, Carl. African Negro Sculptures. ill. 1947   5.50

Klee (Paul) Portfolio of ten color reproductions. 1946 out-of-print

Masson (André) Mythologie de l'Etre. Mythology of Being. ill. 1942   10.00

Moore (Henry) Shelter Sketch Book. ill. 1945 out-of-print

Problems of Contemporary Art. See cover

Rand (Paul) Thoughts on Design. ill. 1947   7.50

Rilke, Rainer Maria. The Sonnets of Orpheus. With nine engravings by Kurt Roesch 1944   90.00

Rodin (Auguste) A la Vénus de Milo. ill. 1946   4.50

Schanker (Louis) Line, Form, Color. Five woodblock color prints. 1944   75.00

Seurat (Georges) by J. Rewald. ill. 1946   6.00

Valentiner, W. R. Origins of Modern Sculpture. ill. 1945   6.00

Vollard, A. Editeur. Catalogue by U. E. Johnson. ill. 1944   18.50

In Preparation:

M. Raymond. From Baudelaire to Surrealism

H. Woelfflin. Principles of Art History

Documents of Modern Art (Director: Robert Motherwell)

d.m.a. 1. **The Cubist Painters (Aesthetic Meditations),** by Guillaume Apollinaire. Edited by Robert Motherwell. Translated from the French by Lionel Abel. 36 pp., 22 small ill., 1944. Out of print. (Revised edition with additional material and corrections in preparation.)

d.m.a. 2. **Plastic Art and Pure Plastic Art,** by Piet Mondrian. Edited by Robert Motherwell. Introduction by Harry Holtzman. 63 pp., 2 color plates, 24 ill., 2nd printing, 1947. $2.25.

d.m.a. 3. **The New Vision,** by Lázló Moholy-Nagy, followed by his autobiographical note, Abstract of an Artist. Edited by Robert Motherwell. Introduction and Obituary by Walter Gropius. Translation completely revised with Moholy-Nagy's approval from the original translation from the German by Daphne Hoffman. 92 pp., 84 ill., 4th revised edition, 1947. $3.00.

d.m.a. 4. **Kindergarten Chats,** by Louis H. Sullivan, with Other Writings. Edited by Isabella Athey. 251 pp., 18 ill., 1947. $4.50.

d.m.a. 5. **Concerning the Spiritual in Art and Painting in Particular,** by Wassily Kandinsky. With Kandinsky's Prose Poems. Edited by Robert Motherwell. Prefaces by Mme. Kandinsky, Julia and Lyonel Feininger, and a contribution by S. W. Hayter. Translated from the German by Sir Michael Sadleir, with revisions by F. Golffing, M. Harrison, and F. Ostertag; prose poems translated by Ralph Manheim. Edition authorized by Mme. Kandinsky, with new footnotes and additions by Kandinsky. 93 pp., 10 ill., 1947. $2.25.

d.m.a. 6. **On My Way,** by Jean (Hans) Arp. Essays and Poems, 1912-1947 in French, German, English. Edited by Robert Motherwell. Translated from the French and German by Ralph Manheim, with 2 woodcuts especially done by the artist for this publication and printed in color, contribution by Carola Giedion-Welcker. Bibliography by B. Karpel. 148 pp., 2 original woodcuts, 48 ill., 1948 $4.50.

d.m.a. 7 **Beyond Painting,** by Max Ernst, with other texts by A. Breton, N. Calas, P. Eluard, G. Ribemont-Dessaignes, T. Tzara and others. Edited by Robert Motherwell. Bibliography by B. Karpel. 220 pp., 140 ill., 1948. $6.00.

d.m.a. 8. **Dada:** An Anthology, texts by Arp, H. Ball, A. Breton, G. Buffet-Picabia, A. Craven, P. Eluard, G. Hugnet, R. Hülsenbeck, G. Ribemont-Dessaignes, H. Richter, K. Schwitters, T. Tzara and others. Edited by Robert Motherwell. Translated from the French and German by Ralph Manheim and others. (First publication in English of most of the material.) 1949.

In active preparation: **Cubism,** by Daniel-Henry Kahnweiler. First translation into English.

The Cubist Painters (Aesthetic Meditations), by Guillaume Apollinaire. Revised edition. (See No. 1 above.)

The Modern Arts in Review. A critical Bibliography compiled and annotated by Bernard Karpel, Librarian, The Museum of Modern Art, New York.

Problems of Contemporary Art

No general editor, being a catch-all for texts relating to the immediate tensions of the arts.

p.c.a. 1. **Form and Sense,** by Wolfgang Paalen. 1945. Out-of-print.

p.c.a. 2. **The Grass Roots of Art,** by Herbert Read. 92 pp., 19 ill., 1947. $1.75.

p.c.a. 3. **The Way Beyond 'Art': The Work of Herbert Bayer,** by Alexander Dorner. Introduction by John Dewey. 244 pp., 154 ill., 7 color plates, 1947. $6.00 (Typography by Herbert Bayer).

p.c.a. 4. **Possibilities: 1.** An occasional Review, edited by John Cage (music), Pierre Chareau (architecture), Robert Motherwell (art), and Harold Rosenberg (writing). Winter 1947-48. Contributions by Abel, Arp, Baziotes, Caffi, Calvo, Paul Goodman, Haieff, Hayter, Hulbeck, Miró, Motherwell, Niemeyer, Poe, J. Pollock, H. Rosenberg, Rothko, David Smith, Virgil Thomson, Varèse, Ben Weber. 112 pp., 49 illus., $2.25 (Typography by the editors).

p.c.a. 5. **Paintings, Sculptures, Reflections,** by Georges Vantongerloo. Preface by Max Bill. 113 pp., 50 ill., 2 color plates, 1948. $3.00.

In active preparation: **Possibilities: 2.** (See No. 4 above.)

Large 8vo. wrappers. Covers and typography (unless otherwise noted) by Paul Rand.

Wittenborn, Schultz, Inc., Publishers. 38 East 57th St., New York 22, New York.